This Comes First!

THIS COMES FIRST!

Bobby H. Welch

BROADMAN
Nashville, Tennessee

All Scripture verses are from the King
James Version of the Bible.

Dewey Decimal Classification: 248.5
Subject heading: WITNESSING
Library of Congress Catalog Card Number: 79-84786
ISBN Number: 0-8054-5504-3

Printed in the United States of America

DEDICATION

*To Maudellen, my wife, who
helps me to put "first things first"*

PREFACE

This book has been written out of the things God has directed through my life and which have made eternal heartprints on me and others who have shared them. Most of this has come from the fire of the pulpit and the give-and-take of my life among the people—those behind the pulpit as well as those in the pew. It is my earnest prayer that this warms your hearts and stirs your souls with a challenge that will motivate to action. It is my hope that Christ can use this book to encourage congregations, Bible classes, individuals, and their acquaintances to do what comes first.

CONTENTS

PART I.

THE PERSONAGE OF JESUS (Acts 1:1-3)

1.	Consistency in Testimony	19
2.	Continuance at the Task	28
3.	Conclusive Test	33

PART II.

THE PROGRAM OF JESUS (Acts 1:4-8)

1.	Personal Program	44
2.	Propagating Program	48
3.	Possible Program	53

PART III.

THE PERIMETER OF JESUS' OPERATIONS (Acts 1:8)

1.	Purpose	63
2.	Passion	65
3.	Provisions	71

PART IV.

THE PREVIEW OF JESUS' RETURN (Acts 1:9-11)

1.	Return	94
2.	Resurrection	98
3.	Reunion	108
4.	Rewards	110

PART V.

THE POWER OF JESUS' CHURCH (Acts 1:12-14)

1.	Vision	122
2.	Vitality	129
3.	Victory	134

This Comes First!

PART I.

THE PERSONAGE OF JESUS

1. CONSISTENCY IN TESTIMONY
2. CONTINUANCE AT THE TASK
3. CONCLUSIVE TEST

THE PERSONAGE OF JESUS

"The former treatise have I made, O Theophilus, of all that Jesus began both to do and teach, Until the day in which he was taken up, after that he through the Holy Ghost had given commandments unto the apostles whom he had chosen: To whom also he shewed himself alive after his passion by many infallible proofs, being seen of them forty days, and speaking of the things pertaining to the kingdom of God" (Acts 1:1-3).

'Coon on a Log

Some years ago *Life* magazine had two pictures which caught the eye in the same publication. The first was a picture of a raccoon on a log in the Ozark Mountains where the 'coon and 'coon dog were chained to the same log and they fought until one killed the other. 'Coon fighting seemed to be a historic mountain sport.

Nearby was a full-page picture of a desperate woman in the very act of suicide. In a fraction of a moment she would be jumping from a sky-scraper building to a New York City sidewalk to end her life. Dr. James Sullivan, former president of the SBC, on seeing this picture, wrote a letter to the editor asking why the photographer did not reach out his hand to catch the arm of this desperate woman. He could have dropped his camera equipment and easily done this to prevent her suicide. Why was he more interested in a dramatic picture than saving her life?

The reply that Dr. Sullivan received from the editor was a sad commentary on our times. He was told that there were thousands of complaints about the 'coon fight, but only one other person in the entire nation had objected to the carelessness of the photographer who was apparently not interested in saving the life of this desperate, suicidal woman. What does this graphic illustration say? It says that many, many in our world are committing their first-rate energies, attentions, affections, and priorities to tenth-rate causes! It is the same inside the life of many churches and individuals today.

What is it that should, and must, claim the first-rate energies, attentions, affections, and priorities of our lives as individual believers and as a collective group called the church? The number-one priority is to be like Jesus, to take on the personage of Jesus who lives within each believer. Our supreme affections and attentions should be given

to the joy of allowing Jesus to live through our
lives.

> Too many of us are living on the right side
> of Easter—and the wrong side of Pente-
> cost.
>
> Too many of us are living on the right side
> of pardon—and on the wrong side of
> power.
>
> Too many of us are living on the right side
> of forgiveness—but on the wrong side of
> fellowship with God.
>
> Too many of us are living outside of Egypt—
> but not living inside of Canaan with a life
> filled with milk and honey.

What comes first in your life? What comes first
in the life of your church? Right now in the space
provided below write in one simple sentence what
comes first with you.

Was it hard to determine? Difficult to word simply? Are you pleased with this priority of life? Does
it "square" with Bible teaching? Would our Lord
be pleased with your priority?

If you hesitated or said "no" or "I am not sure"
to any of these above questions, then this following
study should be exciting and rewarding. If you said
"yes" to all the questions, then you should be

blessed and perhaps even surprised by this study.

The text (Acts 1:1-3) focuses on three basic essentials to living the Jesus-life or taking on the personage of Jesus. Whereas the Gospels show Jesus as the Son of man, the Acts show him as the coming Son of God in the power of the Holy Spirit. The Gospels show what Christ began, while the Acts show what he continued through the Holy Spirit in the life of his disciples. The Gospels tell of the crucified and risen Savior, while the Acts depict him as ascended and exalted Lord and leader. In the Gospels we hear Christ's teachings, but in the Acts we see the effects of his teachings on and through the acts of his disciples and apostles.

While we call the book of Acts "The Acts of the Apostles," it really is the Acts of the Holy Spirit *through* the lives of the followers of Christ. But why is it that we no longer have the power on, and through, our lives and churches as they did in the early church of the Acts? Let us find what God blesses in the book of his acts through his followers and say to ourselves and our churches, "Above all else, this comes first!"

The Personage of Jesus

Regardless of what else happens in us, the most important thing is for us to be like Jesus. Our goal must be Jesus! In the first three verses of Acts 1 our way is clear. The beginning for the child of

God is the day he is saved.

That glorious day when they were born again is not a matter of just joining a church, being baptized, or serving in the activity of the church. All these are vital, but the beginning is when we give our hearts, lives, souls, and livings to Jesus. If we fail here, we fail everywhere. Has there been this salvation-beginning in your life? For a captain who doesn't know where his ship is going, no wind is a good wind. Remember, to fail here is to fail everywhere. To try and go on without this beginning is tragic. But once salvation has been settled, then there are some other steps to taking on the personage of Jesus.

1. CONSISTENCY IN TESTIMONY

"Of all that Jesus began both to do and teach" (verse 1).

We may style our clothing in the best shops, but our testimony must be styled in Jesus. In this first verse Jesus was involved in a divine development. He did not just "begin" and stop. He did not only "do" and fail to share. He did not "teach" that which he was not doing. No! None of that but rather Christ's example is one of consistency of testimony—"*both* to do and teach."

If we, and our churches, are to take on the personage of Jesus, there must be possession to match profession, talk to match walk, works to match words, practice to match preaching, and demonstration to match explanation. As with Jesus, that which has been received must be revealed. This faith of ours must have a life side as well as a lip side. To our religion and redemption there must come to reality a consistency in testimony. The world waits.

> Once it was the blessing; now it is the Lord;
> Once it was the feeling; now it is His Word.
> Once His gifts I wanted; now Himself alone;
> Once I sought for healing; now the Healer own;
> Once 'twas painful trying; now 'tis perfect trust;
> Once a half salvation; now the uttermost.
> Once 'twas what I wanted; now what Jesus says;
> Once 'twas constant asking; now 'tis ceaseless praise;
> Once it was my working; His it hence shall be;
> Once I tried to use Him; now He uses me.
> Once the power I wanted; now the Mighty One;
> Once I worked for glory; now His will alone.

Author unknown

God's Most Embarrassing Question

Those who seek to take on the personage of Jesus find out quickly that obstacles without are nothing compared to hindrances within. The greatest hindrance to our taking on the person of Jesus is simply this—known and unconfessed sin in our lives.

When we talk of *known* sin it means sin that has become a life-style, habit, pattern of life. This sin, or sins, may not be committed daily or even weekly, but it occurs over and over again. It is a sin we have begun to pet and rationalize. We may be calling it our "problem" or "hangup" and not a sin against God. Most often when we commit this sin we are remorseful and desire to be forgiven, even ask for forgiveness, and vow never to commit it again.

However, even as we arise from our knees we have the certain feeling that we'll allow that sin to again rob us of our joy and victory in Jesus. Satan will help us to stay loyal to this known sin by telling us that everyone sins and that even the Bible says so. So why bother to fight sin when it is a hopeless and helpless pursuit! But we must remember that we are not striving for sinless perfection, which is impossible, but rather we are endeavoring to live a life without practicing the same old known sins as a life-style! DON'T EVER FORGET; even if you are victorious over every known sin in your life, you'll still sin enough "accidently" to keep you in the catagory of a *bona fide* sinner, qualifying for the need of God's forgiveness.

Why is this so important? Because serving known sin is robbing us of joy, victory, and power in our daily lives. God tells us that sin cuts us off from him. Read Psalm 66:18, Isaiah 9:2, and Romans 3:23.

Garbage in the Salad

A teenage girl came to her mother who was preparing a tossed salad for the family. The girl began to plead with her mother to let her go to a dance. Then the girl, in unbelief, noticed that her mother was now chopping and tossing bits of garbage into the family salad! The mother graphically explained, "Dear, since you don't care what you allow to affect you spiritually, why should I bother to avoid that which will affect you physically?" Dear friend, known sin is spoiling God's plan and priority for too many Christians and their churches!

In many stores from time to time they will have goods on sale at greatly reduced prices because of fire damage, water damage, irregularity, or the like. Usually the sign to describe these goods reads, "SLIGHTLY SOILED-GREATLY REDUCED." The sign does not read, "SLIGHTLY SOILED—SLIGHTLY REDUCED" but "GREATLY REDUCED!"

In 2 Samuel David is a clear example of how Satan spoils the child of God and what seems at first to be only slightly damaging later leads to great reduction in effectiveness for God. Let's learn a few lessons from this passage.

The Method of Sin

The method of sin is seen in two ways, the timing and the takeover. The timing of Satan on David's life was "when kings go forth to battle David sent Joab." (verse 1) Now it was time for "kings" to go to battle, and David was the king. But David said, "I'll let 'Old George' (Joab) do it for me!" No one can ever take your place or my place in God's army, and you and I must not attempt to allow others to serve God for us. No preacher, missionary, millionaire, teacher, deacon, church, or anyone else can go to war for God in your place. When you allow your ministry to be captured by the armchair and abandon the workshop and warpath for God, just know that Satan is waiting on you. You are in the *wrong* place at the *right* time! Peter says that Satan is like a roaring lion going to and fro seeking whom he shall devour.

The taking in of David by sin and Satan was very subtle. When the timing is right, the taking is easy for Satan! Notice this progression. First, David went out on his own roof, looked over the city, saw a woman, inquired, sent for her—then a child was born! How innocently it all began, out on his own roof, but how very tragically it developed. Satan and sin not only had right timing but made the takeover of a "man after God's own heart," a smooth low-key downfall! Step by step, increment by increment, segment by segment this child of God was rendered ineffective for the Lord.

The Miseries of Sin

Sin always comes out as seen in 2 Samuel 12:14 where Nathan the prophet exposed David. This sin of ours is not hidden. There has never been a perfect crime and never will there be a perfect sin—God knows, and sooner or later it will come out. When sin comes out it always hurts.

Not all suffering is the direct result of sin, but all sin is sure to bring suffering. When someone's child dies it does not mean the parents' sins caused the death. However, David's sin *did* cause his child's death. Sin always hurts when it comes out and sin always comes out! David's life and ministry were affected from that point on. You and I must never forget such vivid lessons as we live, striving for holiness and seeking to take on the personage of Jesus.

The Majesty Over Sin

The method and miseries of sin are real, but God's majesty over sin is all the more real.

I have a book in my library which was given to me by a dear Christian woman. In the strictness of confidence she revealed to my wife and me her sad past. She had become a prostitute after she and her children were abandoned by her husband. This shameful and ungodly way of life had driven her to the end of her rope. She testified that she had sent the children away and had prepared to kill herself. Just as she was at the point of killing herself, a thought out of the past flooded her mind and heart.

Somewhere she had heard about a woman in sin who had been brought to Jesus, and Jesus had forgiven her and said, "Go and sin no more." At that moment this lady thought, "If Christ could do that for her, maybe he can help even me." She said, "I called out for Christ to forgive me and cleanse me and set me free." Then she exclaimed, "He did!" This woman, who is now a pillar of the Lord's work, said, "Pastor, I've told you this that my story might encourage another."

Now, if God can do that for this woman, he can certainly free us from this known life-style sin that deforms our Christian experience and robs us of a consistent testimony and the personage of Jesus.

The Formula to Normality

The reason I have called this the "formula to normality" is: to live above known sin is what God expects in a normal Christian life. The sad fact is that much of Christendom is living sub-normal Christian lives because of known sins. Too many of our new converts have to backslide in order to have fellowship with many of the church! To be a normal, biblical Christian is to live a life of joy, victory, power, and holiness above known sin. Somebody told me that they just wanted to be an average Christian. "Oh no," I said, "average is but to be the worst of the best and the best of the worst, and God has a better plan for you."

I have found, as Tim LaHaye outlines in his book *The Act of Marriage* (page 264), that all known sins of the flesh must be treated the same. The formula that follows will apply to any known sin from prayerlessness to homosexuality. Let me give you some key action words to help us battle known sin:

1. *Face* the sin and name it as a sin. (Stop excusing sin as a problem or hangup).
2. *Confess* it as a sin (1 John 1:9).
3. *Repent* of the sin (Luke 12:3-5).
4. *Accept* Christ as Lord and Savior if you have never done so before (Rev. 3:20, Rom. 10:13).
5. *Ask* God for our victory over this pattern of sin (1 John 5:14-15).
6. *Walk* in the Spirit through daily reading of the Bible and submission to its teachings (Gal. 5:16-25, Eph. 5:17-21, Col. 3:15-17).
7. *Run* from situations and people who would be used of Satan to get you back into this known sin (Rom. 9:12).
8. *Cultivate* wholesome and holy patterns in this area of your life. Do not permit your mind to entertain any alternate idea.
9. *Find* a strong Christian friend who has a victorious life in this area of your struggle and who will keep your confidence. Turn to this

person when the possibility of failure becomes strong.

10. *Remember,* "With men it is impossible but not with God, for with God all things are possible" (Mark 10:27).

The Way Up Is Down

A man watched two goats on a narrow mountain trail. One had started at the top and was headed down. It was the larger goat. The smaller goat had started at the bottom and was headed up toward the top. The two goats would meet at the most narrow part of the path, and it would be absolutely impossible for those two goats to pass at that particular point.

The man who was watching waited to see how this drama would unfold. When the two goats met at the narrow point, at first it appeared that they were going to fight. The large goat, who was headed down, backed up and lowered his head. But then a strange thing happened. As they moved toward each other, the smaller goat got down on its knees, and the larger goat carefully climbed over the small goat. Then the two continued on their way. The larger goat toward the bottom and the smaller goat on toward the top.

To the man who watched, the illustration was clear. *The way up is down.* If we are going to be like the personage of Jesus and maintain a consistency of testimony, we must decide now to have victory over known sin. I have seen the formula just given work in my own life and many, many other lives, and it will work for you, too. But remember, the way up is down!

2. CONTINUANCE AT THE TASK

In this chapter verse 1 speaks of consistency, but verse 2, of continuing. "Until the day in which he was taken up."

Too many of us are "peacock Christians." Like the peacock who has the beautiful array of feathers, we too have to look back in order to see the beauty of God's working on and in our lives. How urgent is the need to be continuing in the *now,* doing that which God has called us to do. The result of continuancy is to glorify the Father and to allow his Son's life to be lived out in us. Our immortality and eternal life are not based on our continuance. For it is not payment of a certain kind of conduct but is the result of a certain kind of character. That certain kind of character is the result of a certain kind of birth. That certain kind of birth is a result of a certain kind of faith. That certain kind of faith is expressed in a certain kind of man. *And that certain kind of man is Jesus.*

Our beginning has everything to do with our continuing, and we cannot be like Jesus unless we continue in that which we began and that to which we are called.

To take on the personage of Jesus requires a consistent testimony, but that testimony must be continuing. Can you imagine what your own personal life would be if you had stayed faithful to those vows you made, soon after conversion, to be a prayer warrior, Bible student, soul winner, church attender, etc.? Can you imagine what your church would be? Your city and the kingdom of God?

Jesus not only "began both to do and to teach" but continued "until the day." What day? Until the day God called him home. Aren't you glad Christ continued and didn't stop in the garden of Gethsemane or on the Jerusalem road to Calvary! The child of God and the church of God are in desperate need of this aspect of the personage of Jesus.

What is it in your life that needs to be renewed or revived? Is it hard for you to continue in this walk with the Lord? What must we know in our effort to be more like Jesus and have continuancy in our task as we walk with him?

General Eisenhower was inspecting his troops minutes before moving to the front lines for a dawn attack. One young wounded soldier was obviously afraid of the dangers ahead. The General tried to encourage the soldier by telling him of all the tanks, planes, firepower that would be supporting them and their attack. Those things did not strengthen the soldier. Then the General moved closer to him and said, "Son, I am scared, too. What if you and I walked up to the front lines together?" Only then did the soldier seem to gain strength and courage and said, "Sir, what I really meant before was that I was afraid earlier, but now I'm OK. I'll make it now."

How is it when we walk with the Lord? Do you remember the two on the road to Emmaus? (Luke 24:13-35). It is apparent these two had allowed their own expectations and preoccupations to rob them of the joy of continuing. Those two had no doubt been in the crowd that cheered Jesus through the streets of Jerusalem at his triumphal entry. (They had the palm fronds—the "I Found It" and "Honk If You Love Jesus" bumper stickers. But what had happened to these two now?) Their expectations had been that of a political and earthly takeover of Jerusalem and the country. They had thought Jesus would do it this way—their way.

We must never lose the power and joy of walking with the Lord when he chooses to do things his way—not our way. Another thing which slowed and sidetracked these disciples, as does with us, was their preoccupation with themselves. How would it look back in their hometown? They had witnessed, testified, gone out on the limb, believed, and it seemed to be all over, as these two thought they could not continue and walk "alone" home. The Bible tells us they were "sad" and headed home, apparently to give up. Now in their self-pity, pride, and ego these previously continuing

Christians had now become cancelled and confused Christians.

A Great Lesson

One of the greatest lessons I have ever learned is this: The worth of a person is determined by but one thing—how *little* it takes to discourage him. Think of that! Don't you know many Christians who are loaded and blessed with gifts, talents, and abilities, but who have been rendered almost completely useless because of some small discouragement? If only they would hang in there and continue, how God could use them!

But because they didn't get their song sung, their name in the church bulletin, their idea accepted, they quit, slow down, and fail to continue. By the way, preachers, church staff members, and deacons are often some of the worst at this! Oh friend, how small a thing does it take to put you out of service and on the shelf? When we walk with the Lord and keep our eyes on him and him alone we will continue until the day!

In this Emmaus passage, even though these disciples' preoccupations and expectations had discouraged them, Jesus was still there and desirous that they become revived, realigned, reconciled, and returned to their continuing for Him. Just because you once did badly does not mean that you should continue to do so. There are only two ways to face life—stop thinking or stop and think. I am told that in many North Carolina weaving mills, where large looms work with thousands of threads, the workers have a sign over their machines. In bold letters the sign reads: "WHEN YOUR THREADS GET TANGLED *STOP* THE MACHINE AND CALL YOUR SUPERVISOR."

Christ wants us to know his will and way for our lives far more than even we want it. These disciples in verses 31 and 32 had their eyes opened. What led to their realizing the presence and the personage of Jesus? They had heard the Bible taught and saw Jesus in "all" the Old Testament. It is confirming to note that the term "Moses and the prophets" is clear evidence that Jesus himself believed in the Mosaic authorship of the first five books of the Bible. And as the Bible was studied, these disciples had talked with Christ. Now that's the road to discovery and maintaining our continuancy in the Word of God—talking with the Son of God!

A Heavenly Heartburn

Look at what happened. "And they said one to another, Did not our heart burn within us while he talked with us by the way, and while he opened to us the scriptures?"

If this heavenly heartburn happened to most of us, we would call for a large bottle of ulcer medicine and send in our reservation for a three-week retreat camp. But these disciples, we are told, reacted to their heavenly heartburn by returning and continuing. "And they rose up the same hour, and returned to Jerusalem . . . Saying, the Lord is risen indeed, and hath appeared to Simon. And they told what things were done in the way . . . (vv. 33-35)

Yes, when Jesus walks with us and we are aware of him and desire to take on his personage, there will be a continuancy about us that will not let us rest on the past or be discouraged in the present.

Concerning the bush which God used to call Moses, one person remarked that it wasn't any sort of special bush—just a willing bush. And it is still true today—"Any old bush will do" (if you and I will continue to let it burn for Christ). But please know that the bush which burns the best catches its fire, as did these disciples, "from the heart."

Vance Havner preached in a message entitled "A Faithful Few on Fire" of reading an ad: "WANTED: wicks, to burn out for God. Oil and lamp supplied." That kind of continuing at the task is required if we are to be like the person of Jesus.

3. CONCLUSIVE TEST

The conclusive test of our lives taking on the person of Christ is only one, as we see in verse 3—showing Jesus alive by "many infallible proofs." This text tells us one of the most gigantic truths of all the Bible—Jesus was showing himself alive! Glory! This is not he who was alive and now is dead, but is Jesus who was dead and is now alive! Hallelujah!

That is precisely the mission of the believer and the church today—to show Jesus alive. This is the need of the world today, to see Jesus alive in us. If we desire to have a godly home, a growing church, a persuasive ministry, then we need to do one thing—show Jesus alive in us. Christ was not merely a witness to the power of God, but he himself was part of the evidence. So it should be with us. Christ-victory is not in our deadness to sin, as important as that is, but the victory is in our being alive in Jesus. Death to sin is negative and removes our penalty, while life in Jesus is positive and gives us our power.

When temptation, injury, and insult come, we can say, "I am dead." When duty, opportunity, challenge, and ministry come, we can say, "I am alive!"

When the Dead Get Loose

There is a wonderful truth in the Bible and it is this: death never has a victory in the presence of Jesus. When death was dedicated to God the presence of Christ brought victory and the new life that was sure to come. This was a physical truth in the Bible and it is now a spiritual truth in our daily living. Consider the cases of Jairus's daughter, the thief on the cross, and, of course, Lazarus.

"For I am persuaded, that neither death, nor life,

nor angels, nor principalities, nor powers, nor things present, nor things to come, nor height, nor depth, nor any other creature, shall be able to separate us from the love of God, which is in Christ Jesus our Lord" (Rom. 8:38-39).

When Jesus came in, death went out to the glory of God. With Lazarus, as well as with others, when the dead got loose the world knew of the victory of Jesus. Now mark this well, there was death and after death there was new life. This truth is still so today.

My Testimony

Grown men were crying—dead men lay twisted and withered. One man, who in two weeks was supposed to be home with his family, lay spent by a bullet between his eyes. There was the smell of gunpowder, sweat, blood, tear gas, and white phosphorus. These were the sights and sounds of battle. But lying ahead just two yards, or two more steps, was where the real battle was going to begin.

I was genuinely saved as a 15½-year-old boy. My salvation had resulted mainly because of my girlfriend who would, after seven years of dating, become my wife. I lived for the Lord and grew in him until college. In high school and then in college I played football and found myself trying to live up to a role image of rough and tough. Soon I found there was little time for the Lord, and I drifted away from him.

I entered the Army as an officer upon college

graduation and attended Airborne, Ranger, and Combat Platoon Leader school, along with Jungle Expert school. At the height of the Vietnam war I volunteered for combat duty. As the helicopter carried me into the jungle of Southeast Asia to become a scout platoon leader, I could never have had any idea of the glorious pilgrimage that was about to unfold.

I have never been unfaithful to my wife and never had a drink of whisky. Even with that you can still do plenty to get you out of the will of God. So there I was—saved but backslidden and out of the will of God.

It had been a bad day. Two men had already been killed, but it would worsen. The call came for my platoon of twenty-eight men to help rescue a company of about 130 men who were pinned down. It seemed impossible, but our platoon had been successful in overrunning eight heavily fortified bunkers and overtaking all the enemy. Well, *almost* all the enemy.

So, there we were in the middle of the sickening sights and sounds of battle. Now only two more yards and I would begin to understand more clearly the truth of "not life to death but death to life." As I took the last of those two steps I glanced to my right, and before I could turn there was fire flashing from the muzzle of a gun. The bullet exploded into my left upper chest and knocked me yards backwards. The bullet tore through my lung, cut my chest muscles in two, and ripped its course, about a pencil lead's width away from my heart, through and out from under my left arm.

As I tried to crawl, fearing another bullet in the back, my ears were ringing, and blood gushed from the softball-size hole in my chest, as well as from my mouth. My men came and tried to help but all in vain—it was all too obvious to everyone, and especially me, that I would die in a matter of minutes. I was certain beyond any shadow of a doubt I would go to be with Jesus, even though I had not lived the life a Christian should have these four years. (By the way, at that time I was of another denomination and had never heard a sermon on eternal security.)

God assured me in those moments before death I was his and he was mine! But there was the most horrifying thing that had overtaken me in those last minutes. *I was embarrassed.* I know it sounds crazy but that was it—embarrassed. I was going to meet Jesus and was embarrassed over the missed opportunities, misplaced priorities, and a life filled with "little" omissions and commissions of sin that had led to a weak and pitiful testimony.

Oh friend, to be embarrassed before Jesus is a terrible thing! I prayed, "God help me." My prayer wasn't for help to live—death was sure—but to clean me up and prepare me to meet Christ, so I would not go in embarrassed, empty-handed, and with a mediocre, misspent life. "God help me" was my soul's cry in the middle of the jungle in the dark of night. I believe God heard that cry. Rather than give me an instantaneous cleanup, he decided to let me live out a new testimony—to live the rest of my life as a postscript!

A helicopter, from no one knows where, landed almost on top of me, and three dead men were put inside, and I was laid on top of them. Through this and several other acts of God, I lived. I had begun to learn now, not of life to death but of death to life. A time later, not in the jungle, but on my knees at my living-room sofa, God was going to teach me the spiritual truth of death to life.

While I was in seminary, each morning during my prayer time, I would kneel at my sofa. One morning it hit me full force—the reality that one must die to live in Christ. Suddenly I grasped my legs and said to God, "Dear Lord, I understand now, these are not really my legs; they are yours. Please take them and use them." Next I did the same with my hands. Then I placed my hands over my eyes and again uttered the same prayer.

I even put my hand on my tongue, and in my heart again said the prayer. Maybe everyone in the world had already discovered what I was discovering that morning, but for me the truth had come alive. The truth was: For me to show Jesus alive would require me first to die in myself and give up to Him. That morning I left that sofa a different person with the certainty that I could and would show Jesus alive. The personage of Jesus had begun to become a reality in my life.

PART II.

THE PROGRAM OF JESUS

1. PERSONAL PROGRAM
2. PROPAGATING PROGRAM
3. POSSIBLE PROGRAM

THE PROGRAM OF JESUS

"But ye shall receive power, after that the Holy Ghost is come upon you: and ye shall be witnesses unto me . . ." (Acts 1:8).

Early each morning a foreman stopped at a clock shop across from the mill where he worked. He would always be sure to set his watch to match the time of the big old grandfather clock in the watchmaker's show window.

One morning as the foreman came to set his watch, he found the old clock, that had been there many, many years, gone. He burst into the shop, asking about the whereabouts of the clock.

"Why are you so concerned?" asked the owner.

The foreman said, "I am responsible for sounding the work whistle for all the men at the mill, which tells them when to begin and stop work, and the whistle regulates much of our town. All these years I have depended upon your big clock for the correct setting."

The watchmaker stroked his chin in deep thought, and then spoke this pregnant sentence. "Isn't it a strange world? You see, all these years I have been setting my clock by the mill whistle that you sound."

Oh, that is the case of the program of many of our own lives and our churches! We are simply setting our lives to each other's programs and so often miss the victory of getting in on what God is up to.

One of the most stupid statements that so strikingly resembles good sense is to say, "We are doing as well as they are doing." We are to march to the beat of Christ's drum and to it alone! To us many programs are introduced, but we simply must know the program of Jesus and repeat to ourselves and our churches, "This comes first!"

Religious activities are not always Christ's program. May I remind us that the most active chicken is usually the one which has just lost its head. So often we become too busy doing church work that we fail to do the work of the church. We realize that the church is the body of Christ to carry on the mission of Christ here on this earth. So then, to know what we are to carry on is to know what Jesus began and died to continue.

What was the program of Jesus? Nothing is any clearer in all of the Bible than this. "For the Son of man is come to seek and to save that which was lost" (Luke 19:10). "Even as the Son of man came not to be ministered unto, but to minister, and to give his life a ransom for many" (Matt. 20:28). "This is a faithful saying, and worthy of all acceptation, that Christ Jesus came into the world to save sinners; of whom I am chief" (1 Tim. 1:15).

Dr. Paul Meigs related the story of a boy who had just gotten a new hat. The boy was playing with friends in a game of "follow the leader" while wearing his new hat. Suddenly the boy, who could not swim, fell into a well where the water was over his head. The new hat floated atop the water while the little fellow faltered for his life beneath its surface. The boy's little sister ran frantically to the house, crying and screaming at the top of her voice to her parents, "Mother, Mother, Daddy, Daddy, come quick—Bubba's new *hat* is in the water!!"

Many of our lives and our churches's lives are programed to rescue Bubba's hat, but it is Bubba himself that God is concerned about!! Do we have the orthodox program that satisfies the intellect and interest but fails to touch the lives of a lost and dying world? To see lost people saved is the number-one priority of the church and its people.

There is a legend that tells of Jesus, after his ascension into heaven, talking with an angel. The angel asked, "Since you are no longer on earth, dear Lord, what is your plan that the lost might know of you and the Father?"

To this, the legend says, Jesus answered, "Why, I have told my followers to tell them of me."

The angel, knowing something of the earthly Christians, replied, "But what if they fail to do this, what then is your plan?"

At that Jesus looked straight into the angel's face and, with tears in his eyes, said, "They must not fail at this, for this is my *only* plan."

We are God's plan to reach a lost and dying world. The program of Jesus must be our program. For this program to be Jesus' program it must be personal, propagative, and powerful. And I might add that the remedy for a sick church is to put it on an evangelism diet because, as John Wesley said, "We have but one business . . . to save souls."

1. PERSONAL PROGRAM

Verse 8 is the key verse to the entire book of "The Acts of the Holy Spirit" through the lives of the disciples. The reason: the two words "witness" and "Holy Spirit" being brought together in this one verse.

The word "witness" is used over thirty times, while Holy Spirit is used over seventy times. Here in this one verse these two dominant expressions are combined to tell the believer what should personally characterize his individual life-style. Isn't it so obvious and glorious that the program of Jesus includes us in a personal manner? "You" gives us a personal duty and privilege to be co-laborers with Christ! It is true that Christ alone can save the world, but Christ cannot save the world alone. "You" are vital to the program of Jesus.

Jesus said, "Follow me, and I will make you fishers of men." There are two sides to this coin. One, if we are truly following Jesus we personally will be fishing for souls. Two, if we are not personally fishing for souls we are not really following Jesus.

We may do many other good things while fishing for souls and thus be following Jesus. However, we can do every good thing and not fish for souls and thus fail to follow Jesus. Being a personal witness is not a gift only given to a few, but rather a command and responsibility for every child of God. Our responsibility as witnesses is not a cafeteria-style obligation, but it is served to us on a "thus-saith-the-Lord" order. "Ye shall be . . ."

I think the theology is a little weak, but the point is very strong in this little poem.

Sittin' by the Fire

He wasn't much for stirring about
It wasn't his desire
While others went out witnessing
He was sittin' by the fire.

The same old thing day after day
He never seemed to tire
While others went out witnessing
He was sittin' by the fire.

Alas, he died as all men do
Some say he went up higher
But while others went out witnessing
He was sittin' by the fire.

Author unknown

Personal witness cannot be relegated to the long-range bombardment of our pulpits and missions offerings but must also involve "you" in the hand-to-hand and heart-to-heart struggle for souls in the trenches of daily living. Would you time yourself for five minutes and write down five names of lost people for whom you are praying to be saved.

(1) _____
(2) _____
(3) _____
(4) _____
(5) _____

The first time I did this, I believe those were the five longest minutes of my life. The point is that until we know and are praying for lost people we are not going to take personally Jesus' program of witnessing. The devil will make us want to cry out, "Am I my brother's keeper?" You and I must remember that this line of reasoning began by a man who was too religious to slay a lamb, but who was not close enough to God to keep from killing his own brother (Gen. 4:9).

Two of the finest Christian men I have ever

known recently gave their testimonies at our church's weekly visitation supper. They told of having an assignment of visiting a prospect whom we had found during a door-to-door survey. They had a hard time finding the house, and the prospect's neighbor said the woman for whom they were searching was of very questionable reputation. The possibility seemed useless, and both men felt that it was really worthless even to go to the door, but they went ahead and knocked.

When the woman came to the door the men, feeling the uselessness of much pursuit, asked if she attended church anywhere. She answered, with a troubled voice, that she had before, but not a Baptist church. Both men dropped the conversation at that. As they left the door they wrote "NO PROSPECT" across the assignment card. Then the younger of the two men, who was giving his testimony, pulled out a newspaper article and began to read. It told of a woman who had just that morning committed suicide by hanging herself in the bathroom. It was the woman at the door!

"We were wrong," wept the men, "to ever write 'NO PROSPECT' and give up without asking her about her relationship with Christ." She wasn't interested in church, but what she needed then and there was Jesus. What a moving moment that was as others and I personally committed ourselves to this responsibility of witnessing in the power of the Holy Spirit.

It is easy to see the reasoning behind Spurgeon's

statement to his "preacher boys." He admonished them, "If I had one wish for you, it would be that you could spend sixty seconds in hell—then no one would ever have to try and convince you of its reality or encourage you to win souls."

A man asked of a little boy, who seemed to have more apple than he could eat, "Too much apple for a little boy?"

The boy replied, "No sir, just not enough boy for this apple!"

Today we have enough religion to sink the world, but the problem is we don't have enough Christians taking their witnessing personally enough to save the world! God had only one son, and he made him a doorstep evangelist. Jesus took this responsibility personally and so should you and I.

2. PROPAGATING PROGRAM

When a Christian takes his responsibility personally he will soon make sure that the gospel will be spread by his witness. The first work of the whole church is to carry the gospel to every person in the whole world.

I heard of a woman who was becoming a little

disturbed over the fact that she was getting along in years and hadn't found a husband. So she went to her pastor about it. He said, "Well, you know that the Lord has a program—one man for one woman and one woman for one man. That is God's program, and you can't improve on that." She replied, "I don't want to improve on it—I just want to get in on it."

God's program of witnessing is for the whole world to know about Jesus and for each Christian to be busy telling. The word translated "witness" is the same word which means "martyr." The early Christians who took Jesus seriously concerning witnessing became martyrs. Especially was this so immediately after Pentecost.

Some were boiled to death in oil, some were skinned alive and left to die, some were covered with tar and set afire as torches around Caesar's palace. Others were dragged to death by wild horses, some were eaten by wild animals, some were sawn in two, and then some literally rotted to death in prison. The blood of that type of Christian witness has, and always will be, "the seed of the church."

In light of such "a cloud of witnesses," Christ must be ashamed of how so many of us shy away in the face of great opportunities to witness. Ours is the joy of telling the glad tidings of Jesus. The more Godless a city, the greater the need for a Christian to witness. A Christian who is too thin-skinned to face lost mankind and witness for Jesus is not fit to lead a Bible class, serve as a deacon or as a pastor, or lead the Lord's army. How can a Christian who sniffles witness effectively for Jesus? We need to stop our pining, moping, brooding, and excusing, and take up the joyful language of the early church who witnessed, "Jesus saves!"

We are to be nothing less and nothing more than gospel "newspaper boys." Our responsibility is to put the good news of Jesus at every doorway. In so doing we must guard that we do not so "flower" it up that it becomes mistaken for a yard plant. Also, we must be careful that we don't make it so sophisticated and high sounding that it goes over the lost man's head and lodges on the roof. (When we shoot over the heads of our listeners, the only thing it proves is that we can't aim.) No sir, we are to put the good news at the door where it can easily be found and understood.

Now some will say, "God bless you, gospel newsboy!" A few others will say, "Be gone with you and your news!" But no matter what is said, our task is to deliver the good news.

I remember an evangelism teacher in seminary saying, with tears in his eyes, something I will never forget. "Boys, after you have seen, as I have, a few of your loved ones go out into eternity without Jesus as Savior you'll stop worrying about using cultivative evangelism or being misunderstood." Selective, sophisticated, and cultivative evangelism can become dangerous delaying devices in our attempts to witness boldly.

A lost man was dying when his Christian friend of over twenty years came to the bedside. The Christian told the dying man what a wonderful and abundant life Christ had given him over his many years as a Christian. Further, he told the dying man of his (the Christian's) own certainty of a wonderful home in heaven and the escape of hell. Finally he encouraged this lost and dying friend to accept Jesus as Savior now before it became too late. Suddenly, the dying man arose on one elbow and shouted, "It's a lie, it's got to be a lie! Because if all this is true, and you had really been my friend all these years, you would never have waited this late to tell me. It's got to be a lie!"

What a lost and dying world needs is Jesus and they need him *now*. Too many of our churches are filled with Christians who are too heavenly minded to be any earthly good. We are to be as a ship's captain with our eyes on heaven but our hands on the helm, with our head in the stars but our feet on the deck. There is one thing we cannot do in heaven that must be done here, and that is winning the lost.

A little girl, wanting some candy, came to her busy father. In hopes of delaying his little girl he took a page on which there was printed a map of the world and tore it into many pieces. He presented it as a puzzle to be reassembled by the little girl. In only a few moments she was back with the world picture put together perfectly. The father was astonished at how quickly she got it all back together and asked how. She replied, "There was a picture of a man on the backside, and when I got the man put together, the world was put back together." That is exactly why the church and Christians should agree on winning anyone anywhere they can. If the man is put together right, the world will be, too.

But isn't it amazing how churches and preachers can argue over where and who to win because of their so-called "church fields"? I was a lifeguard for five years and saw some who appeared to be dead come back to life after they had been rescued from sure death in the water. Often it would take several lifeguards to rescue one person from the water. But I never heard one of those rescued people tell us we had too many lifeguards after them or that some of the lifeguards should have stayed somewhere else. No, they were thankful that one and all put every effort forth to rescue them from their perishing. And dear friend, the soul that is rescued from eternal perishing isn't going to fuss over church fields and the like, either. We need to stop allowing Satan to sidetrack us "lifeguards" from our number-one program. Today too many "lifeguards" are on the shore discussing while the multitudes are in the water perishing.

3. POSSIBLE PROGRAM

This personal and propagating program of Jesus is a possible program for one reason and one reason alone, the power of God's Holy Spirit.

You know, of course, that it is the Holy Spirit who does the warning, wooing, and winning of souls. Witnessing is the supreme result of the power of the Holy Spirit upon our lives; nothing else is mentioned in this key passage. The objective of witnessing is the salvation of souls.

Oswald Smith, in his book, *Enduement of Power* (page 58), brings into perspective this power that makes the program possible. "Therefore great results follow the anointing, for evidences that can neither be disputed nor counterfeited. The first is victory over sin; the second, power in service; third, fruit of the Spirit and fourth, a burden for souls. Now I care not what else you may have received, even though visions and revelations have been yours—they fade into insignificance in the face of these four tremendous results.

"Have you, then, the burden? Do you weep over souls? Are you longing to see them saved? Do you value all meetings insofar as they contribute to the salvation of sinners? Do you judge the spirituality of a church by its interest in the saving of lost men and women?"

The Holy Spirit is the key to giving the burden that in turn makes the program possible.

Just as sure as the Holy Spirit makes the program possible, there is another often-overlooked key. That key is joy. Now, you ask, what does joy have to do with spreading the gospel? Everything! This point is where most of us, and our churches, lose the momentum of witnessing and thus see the program become impossible.

Here is the point: most of us are prepared to have joy when a soul is won but are discouraged when our witness does not produce immediate fruit. Usually we have much praise for some witness who gives testimony of seeing a person come to Christ but have scarcely any commendation for the witness who had just been faithful to witness, in spite of a lack of fruit. Joy should come over just giving a witness in the power of the Holy Spirit with, or without, immediate fruit. The farmer loves to work the soil and finds immense joy in the labor—in season and out of season. Such a farmer is happy, productive, and ultimately successful.

Since the Holy Spirit is responsible for success in souls, and we are to be faithful, let us learn to rejoice in sowing the precious seed of the gospel. I challenge you to begin rejoicing over your own witnessing, as well as that of others, and see if there is not a dynamic change in your witnessing power. It is true that the Lord gives you some you do not go after, because you do not get some you do go after. This is the truth because it is the Holy

Spirit's responsibility to make Jesus' program possible throughout a personal, propagative witness.

We find our part in Christ's program like that of the little boy whose mother overheard him giving God some instructions during his prayers. The mother told the boy, "Son, don't bother to give God instructions—you just show up for duty!"

I had rather fail in a program that is going to ultimately win than to win in a program that will ultimately fail. Jesus' program is possible and will be victorious, but we are to be faithful whether it appears we are immediately fruitful or not. You see, it is impossible to give the gospel to the wrong person!

In spite of all this, it is still easy to become discouraged because so many to whom we witness never come forth as believers. Jesus has an encouraging lesson in the parable of the sower.

When it comes to our program and the programs of our churches, we must keep our vision clear. Because a man or a church without clearness of Jesus' program is likely to be led to organize a new group, committee, society, or fellowship, or the like. This can happen because such can give a person with no aim an opportunity to appear to be doing something when he is doing nothing.

Many communities, churches, and Christians are always ready to mistake the multiplication of "wheels" for an increased speed in the progress of the Lord's chariot. In all likelihood, half the distraction within our churches today would not be in existence were it not for idled and fuzzy brains of people who care more for the manipulation of machinery than for the accomplishment of spiritual ends in the saving of souls. It will be a most tragic day when a church or believer climbs to the top of the ladder and finds the ladder has been leaning against the wrong wall. Jesus' program must come first!

A preacher and his young son were returning home after a meeting in a distant city. As they were traveling along, a car passed them on a hill. There was the squeal of tires, the crash of steel, and the sound of broken glass as an approaching car collided headon with the car that had passed the pastor and his son.

When they could no longer be of help, the pastor and his son continued homeward. For the remainder of the trip the boy sat stunned, seemingly reliving the experience over and over. The screams of agony and the dying of the occupants of that car had made a tremendous impression on the boy. The father was concerned, not only about the eternal destiny of the people who had died, but also about his impressionable son who had witnessed such a horrible disaster.

Naturally the boy could not eat when they arrived home. He went to bed early. The father became even more concerned about his son for the boy still had not spoken. In the middle of the night the young boy cried aloud. His father went to his aid. The father asked, "Son, can't you sleep?" The boy replied, "Daddy, when men die how can *we* sleep!"

Napoleon with most of his men dead or wounded was caught in a seemingly hopeless battle and called to his bugler to sound a retreat. The bugler called back, "Sir, you never taught me to sound a retreat, but I can blow a 'charge' that will raise the dead!" He did and Napoleon's troops rallied and won.

Jesus never taught us a "retreat" when it comes to personal witnessing. We need a "charge" that will wake the dead and revive hearts to the spreading of the gospel as the program of Christ and our churches lives. *This comes first!*

Part III.

THE PERIMETER OF JESUS' OPERATIONS

1. PURPOSE

2. PASSION

3. PROVISIONS

THE PERIMETER OF JESUS' OPERATIONS

". . . and in Jerusalem, and in all Judaea, and in Samaria, and unto the uttermost part of the earth" (Acts 1:8).

When you have taken on the personage of Jesus this leads naturally to the program of Jesus. But where is it that we should activate this program of witnessing in the power of the Holy Spirit?

I have used the word "perimeter" because that means a circle. When we take this passage of Scripture seriously it tells us that we are to go from Jerusalem to Judea, to Samaria, to the uttermost part of the world, which means to cover the entire known world. Doing what? Witnessing in the power of the Holy Spirit. That's right, around the world! The first work of the Holy Spirit is to get the gospel into the whole world.

The Uncancelled Commission

"Go ye therefore, and teach all nations, baptizing them in the name of the Father, and of the Son, and of the Holy Ghost: Teaching them to observe all things whatsoever I have commanded you: and lo, I am with you alway, even unto the end of the world. Amen" (Matt. 28:19-20).

My first mission in Vietnam, as a scout platoon leader, was to track down about 300 infantry groups, using as a guide a wounded enemy prisoner. My commanding officer said, "These are your orders." Since I had only twenty-eight men, the odds did not look good at all. Remember, this was my first mission!

I will never ever forget the relief that I felt when over my radio came a second set of orders to supercede the first, "mission cancelled." Whew! Our whole platoon began to loosen our equipment, lay our weapons aside, and even relax. That's the way you do when the mission is cancelled.

From the way many of us use our equipment, lack a sense of urgency in our affairs, and seem to be "at ease in Zion," it appears we must have heard some superceding orders to counteract our great commission from God. If you have gotten such an idea, it certainly did not come from God because his commission for world evangelism is an uncancelled commission!

I heard of a father who, unaccustomed to a family shopping schedule, had forgotten and left his son standing outside a department store. He had told his son to stay right in that spot until he got all the packages into the automobile. But in the father's haste he had climbed right into the car and driven out of the lot, leaving the son behind. Suddenly the father remembered what he had done, turned around, and headed back. About that time a fierce rain began to fall. The father found his son soaking wet from the top of his head to the soles of his feet, waiting outside the store.

The father asked the boy, "Son, why didn't you get back into a dry place until I came?"

And the boy replied simply, "Well, father I stayed exactly where you told me to stay until you came back for me!"

Our heavenly Father has told us exactly what we should be doing until he comes back for us, and the uncancelled commission is still in effect for world evangelism. We need to stay there until our Father comes for us!

How Can You Know?

There are some things which indicate if a Christian and a church are taking seriously their commission to evangelize the world.

1. PURPOSE

I have already discussed what should be the top priority of the Christian in his church. That purpose is to see people saved, but the purpose ultimately should be to affect the whole world. That is what Jesus said, and I am certain that he meant exactly that—the world. The last thing Jesus said on earth to the church was "go!" The first thing Jesus said in heaven to the Holy Spirit was "go!" Both of these commissions were for one thing— world evangelism!

Our church fields should be no smaller than a nation and no larger than the existing continents! For us to affect continents we must set our purpose beyond a church building on a corner. So often people are busy building many institutions, but Christ was busy building one thing—a church of born-again persons. To be sure, there is a place for buildings and institutions, but there is only one purpose for them, and that is world evangelism.

There was a lighthouse keeper who was without proper help to keep the grounds, to paint the buildings, and to go for supplies. The keeper became busy tending to these matters, and a ship crashed on the rocks. A government agent came to investigate the cause, and, of course, the keeper told all of his problems. Then the agent looked at him and said, "But your job was to keep the light burning for the ships!"

And to us that does not mean home port ships alone but foreign port ships as well. What is the purpose of your church? *If it does not have the earnest intent to win the entire world it will not do what it should in winning your community.*

A young boy fishing kept throwing all of his big fish back in and keeping the little ones only. When asked why he was doing such, he replied, "Well, all I can handle are the small ones because my skillet is small, only ten inches in size." Now I am afraid that is why many of us are not reaching out farther—because we have equipped ourselves with small expectations. What can be done about that? We must ask God to give us a real passion for people.

2. PASSION

Passion for souls must be real if we are to see world missions and world evangelism become a reality.

In 1953 the world's highest mountain, Everest, was conquered. But perhaps not many of us remember that three years before that another mountain in the Himalayas, the first to be scaled in the 26,000-foot class, was conquered by Maurice Herzog and his companion. When Herzog stood at the top of Annapurna, he turned to his companion and said, referring to the rest of the climbing party down at the different camps along the way, "Oh, if only the others could know!" But then he added, "If only the whole world could know."

Jesus after the resurrection was standing on a much higher plain than Annapurna. He had conquered sin and death, holding the key to all eternity. He said to his disciples, "As the Father hath sent me, even so I send you" (John 10:21). Christ's passion was that "the whole world must know!"

Some way the church and the child of God must take on the passion of Paul as seen in Romans 1:14-17. In this passage there are three vital "I ams" that must be present to engender a real passion for souls.

"I am debtor" (v. 14). Too many of God's people, and even God's preachers, feel like the world owes them something. That is not so—the entire world doesn't owe you a living; you owe the entire world a life. A life that reaches a world for Christ. Much of our world evangelism fails because churches of God and men of God start thinking in terms of what they can get rather than what they would give. When the church ceases to be a debtor, it stops being effective, especially in world evangelism. Paul had people on his heart, not property, pleasure, prestige, and there resulted passion on his ministry! We are debtors because we have a personal knowledge of Christ. Because we have a knowledge of the world's ignorance of Christ. Because we have the knowledge of how to bring a world to Christ!

A little girl's playmate had just died, and the little girl's father told her not to visit the bereaved mother's home that day. But the little girl did go over to the home of her dead friend's mother. When she came back home the frustrated father asked, "Now, how could you have helped any by going over to that poor brokenhearted mother?" Then his little girl spoke volumes as she replied, "Well, I just crawled up in her lap and helped her cry."

Dear friend, an aching and sinsick world is waiting for someone to come and sympathize and share an answer to their hurting hearts. Untold millions are still untold, and we debtors have a worldwide obligation to tell.

"I am ready" (v. 15). What keeps us from being ready? Sometimes it is the fear of failure. It was said of John Knox: "He feared God so much he had no room to fear man." This same spirit should carry over into every area of our lives and ministry where there are threats to impeding our zeal for world evangelism. Paul in Philippians 2:10-11 declares that there shall come that day when every knee shall bow and every tongue shall confess that Jesus is Lord. Therefore, the church of the living God needs to stand up and say "I am ready" with the gospel. Paul was ready to put the gospel to its most severe test. And for all practical purposes it would be on the "foreign" soil of Rome.

In Rome, it would meet the greatest religious test, for it would come to grips with paganism.

In Rome, it would meet the greatest political test,

for it would come to grips with imperialism.

In Rome, it would meet the greatest social test, for it would come to grips with a city's motley mob.

In Rome, it would meet with its greatest moral test, for it would come to grips with a nation's vast criminality.

But Paul was ready, whatever the test. Do you have the passion that makes you ready? Are you ready for Rome, at home, and around the world with the gospel? Are you ready to be a voice for world evangelism? World evangelism needs ready people more than rich people or brilliant people or big people.

After my military obligation, my wife and I built and operated our own business and became active lay people in our church. Our business had us $40,000 in debt and we had a new baby girl that made us even more aware of our obligations.

A foreign missionary named Shelby Smith had come back from Ecuador and was preaching in our church. His wife had died on the mission field. At the end of one service, Dr. Smith put his wife's shoes on the altar. Then he made a statement to this effect: "My wife, after her death, stepped out of these very shoes and vacated a spot in world missions and evangelism: Now is there someone who is ready to step into them for Christ's sake around the world?"

At that moment God began a call in my heart to reach souls wherever and whenever. Shortly after that experience I was in a darkened back bedroom of our home. I was praying with my head buried in the end of the bed with both fists tightly clenching handsful of the spread.

For me to stop what I was doing and obligate myself to go reach people for Christ was impossible, it seemed. My prayer was, "Dear Lord, if it takes burning my business to the ground, or whatever, so I might be free to do your will, please do it—because whatever the cost I am ready." God answered that prayer. Although he did not burn the business down he did free me in every way. A few months later I had leased our business, sold our Buick, given some furniture away, and dropped our plans for the dream home into the wastebasket, and prepared to follow Jesus wherever the perimeter of his operation required.

With the remainder of our furnishings packed into a U-Haul truck, my wife and baby in the seat beside me, we were soon lost in the dark of night as we pulled away from our home. We thought *What is causing us to do this?* But one thing—we were ready to share our gospel with a passion for souls. We were not the best equipped, not the smartest, not the most gifted, but we were ready. Oh, even now I do earnestly pray that the "I am ready" which burned in my heart for souls that day will never leave me or my ministry. Dear God, give us souls for world evangelism.

"I am not ashamed" (v. 16). For some to be ready

is one thing and to be bold in spreading the gospel and not ashamed seems to be another. But there are at least two great reasons we are not to be ashamed. One, "for it is the power of God unto salvation" (v. 16). World evangelism is not a matter of race or place but the power of God's grace. Two, "for therein is the righteousness of God revealed. . . . " (v. 17). Here is a glimpse of the power of world evangelism in that this is the basis for the release of God's power through us into a lost world.

We understand clearly why everyone of us should see our place as a debtor, ready and not ashamed, as we examine W. Griffith Thomas's suggestions about the remarkable elements of verse 17:

1. The *source* of the gospel—"God"
2. The *nature* of the gospel—"Power"
3. The *purpose* of the gospel—"Salvation"
4. The *scope* of the gospel—"Everyone"
5. The *reception* of the gospel—"Believeth"
6. The *efficiency* of the gospel—"Therein is the righteousness of God revealed . . ."
7. The outcome of the gospel—"The just shall live by faith."

The gospel of Jesus in one way is like a lion in the jungle—no one has to convince anyone that the lion is king—just turn him loose, and he will prove it. What a gospel! What a Savior! What a world in need! What a passion we should have for souls!

3. PROVISIONS

Even with our purpose clearly defined and our passion for souls stirred and lastingly within us, there still must be provisions made for world evangelism.

Now, within ourselves and our churches, we can never provide provisions equal to the opportunity of world evangelism. This is precisely why the personage of Jesus must be real in our lives before program and perimeter will ever be possible. We must have God's resources. However, be aware that we as human instruments will still be the channels of God's resources.

If the account of Jesus' feeding the multitude with the loaves and fishes from the lad tells us anything, it should be that the Lord is our source.

A boy working with his father was trying to move a large rock by himself. Finally in despair he said, "It is no use—it can't be moved." Then his father said, "Son, don't ever say it cannot be done until both you and your father have tried together." At that, both boy and father easily moved the large rock. It's the same with the provisions for world evangelism and world missions. God says, "All power is given unto me in heaven and in earth" (Matt. 28:18). And that guarantees power for provisions to win the world.

Prayer

Prayer is a must before all other provisions. All of our provisions and activities can yield something, but when we really rely on prayer we get what God can yield. We must realize our helplessness to produce Godly results. To be sure, man can organize, deputize, supervise, agonize, and build what even appears to be a church. But to have something brought down rather than have something worked up comes from prayer that moves the hand of God. As one writer put it, "The power of prayer is no more or less than the mighty power of God released through the life of a man who stops being an obstacle of God. The power is God's alone" (*Prayer and Pretense* by John Hanne, 1974, Grand Rapids, Michigan: Zondervan Corp., p. 44).

I remember well the second revival I ever preached. For no reason at all I told God I wanted to see at least seven souls saved on the first morning, which was Easter Sunday. The crowds came, the music and message were present, but in both meetings of the day there was one lone rededication.

On the next day the old pastor of the church, where I was preaching, had invited some prayer partners to meet with us in the morning to pray. Since I had been a part of the prayer meeting for souls before, I felt free to make plans for later in the morning, allowing an hour for the prayer time. We met about ten—there was little talk of anything.

The old pastor said, "Men, we need the power of God on this preacher and our services that souls might be saved." At that announcement the men began to pray. They did not pray sentence prayers, each taking their turn until all had something, and then dismiss the meeting. No, these men would each pray long and often, again and again, after someone else had prayed. Sometimes there would be a prolonged lull in the voices, twenty or more minutes of no one praying but whispers to God from first one and then another. But at such lulls in the praying nobody seemed to know to dismiss us and no one seemed to have pressing business for the remainder of the morning.

After a bit the men would pray more—no sense of vain repetition but fresh soul-searching, and often aimed directly for my anointing to preach and plead for souls. Once I opened my eyes to see the men had abandoned fashionable postures of prayer and one by one made them a place before God. Eyeglasses and wristwatches were laid aside; one man sat on the floor against the door. The old pastor was under his desk, lying flat on the floor, and I could see only his arm. These men had come to stay and pray and meet with God. I felt like an onlooker at Jacob's wrestling with the angel. There were none of these hyperemotional "tongues."

Some way the meeting finally stopped, and now it was hours later into the afternoon. We would now give ourselves to personal work for the remainder of the day. As we left, the men agreed to meet each day to pray. I preached that night with new power but with no outward results at all. After the services several men of the church, with the lanterns, met me and we went out on a mountain—climbed a log ladder and got into a small cave to pray and plead again for souls.

Each day we prayed this way—each night I would preach to larger and larger crowds, but for four days not one soul came forward. Then on the fifth night 127 people came forward, almost all for salvation, and in the next two days over 250 people responded to the call of Christ. Why? Not because of my telling God I wanted seven souls but because of men who knew how to pray. There was nothing fancy, just men after God or God after men, as I think back it must have been both! In those days God began to teach me the worth of a soul and the power of prayer.

Someone has said, "Prayer is a cannon aimed to burst open the gates of glory!" How true that is, but the cannon must be fired by human hands and hearts.

There must be collective praying, but it will be no stronger than individual praying. Prayer at its best is love for souls on its knees. A Christian can stand taller and go further on his knees than any other way. We find that kneeling always keeps us in good standing with God.

Harold Lindsell explains, "Distance is no bar, space no barrier, to reaching the remotest place on earth. Nor is the power of prayer diminished by the distance between the person who prays and the person who is prayed for. Men and nations can too have their destinies decided by God's praying people who, through intercessory prayer, wield power greater than the armed might of the nations of the earth" (*Pray-Read the Word* by Witness Lee, Los Angeles, California: Stream Publishers, pp. 52-53).

Matthew 18:20 gives us the secret to prayer—"There am I." It doesn't matter where we are or how difficult and demanding the circumstances, "there" is where Jesus will meet us if we pray. The meeting may be over a sick pet, a Communist nation, or a quest for world evangelism, but "there" Jesus will meet us.

The personal pronoun "I" tells us this will be a personal meeting by none other than God's only Son. Personal attention is given to our prayer by Almighty God through Jesus. To have this promise should cause us all to hurry to our prayer closets. Collective praying such as we have throughout our churches is much needed—they will never be any stronger than our individual prayer lives. The question is, "Do you pray?" Is there that time when you meet regularly and personally alone with the Lord?

Let me suggest Stephen Olford's little booklet, *Manna in the Morning,* as well as *Change the World's School of Prayer* manual. Both are excellent helps for the Christian who hungers to meet daily with the Lord.

I have found that there are some key elements to maintaining a meeting with the Master. *First, there needs to be a specific time set aside.* This time needs to be regarded as holy. At all cost we must not allow this time to be hindered. When others ask for this time we must tell them, "I have another appointment that is critical!" This time could be any time, but it needs to be the same time day by day.

Next, there needs to be a special time where you will not be interrupted. After all, God Almighty is going to talk to you, and you won't want to miss a word. This place could be any place, but it needs to be the same place day by day. The less of the world that is in this place, the less you will be distracted from God.

After the time and place, then *there must be caution exercised* because we are so easily stopped from praying. I have found that if I pray on my knees for very long I begin to go to sleep, especially in the morning, so I walk while I pray. I walk from one side of the room to the other. Also, I have learned to pray aloud so my mind will not wander to other thoughts.

Needless to say, if a person is going to walk and pray aloud he needs to keep his eyes open. You know what, even with my somewhat strange habits, I have found God willing to meet with me day by day, hearing and answering my prayers. Some of the most glorious mornings of my life have not been preaching to thousands but meeting with God, barefoot on the cold concrete of my garage, walking wall to wall in my pajamas, Bible under my arm, talking to the Father.

This brings us to the big problem in prayerlessness, and that is self-discipline. We talk so freely of the Lordship of Christ, but lay prayerless and powerless because of the lack of self-discipline with the Lord. I am thinking of times of sharing a room in a motel with fellow preachers and having to go out into the woods or maybe a nearby walkway in the blowing cold rain to get alone with God.

Someone asked the great prayer warrior George Müller if he would pray for them to get up out of the bed in the morning so they would pray. Müller said, "Only after you have got one foot on the floor yourself will I pray for God to help you get the other foot on the floor."

We have a part ourselves in getting to the meeting place with God. Whatever the cost—whether, loss of sleep, misunderstanding, suffering—we must day by day get alone with God! Many, I am sure, are like me—no sooner do I get my personal prayer altar built than something comes along to hinder, distract, and even destroy my time alone with the Father. God help us to be found day by day rebuilding, for as long as necessary, our prayer altar in order to meet with God.

Pray when you will, how you will, where you will, but pray, brother, pray! You and I may never go personally to a home or foreign mission station but we can be prayer missionaries. E. M. Bounds said, "Our one great business is prayer and we will never do it well unless we fasten to it with blinding force" (*The Reality of Prayer* by E. M. Bounds, 1961). And I would further add that world evangelism will never be done until by binding force it is fastened to our one great business of prayer.

People

People provision is one that is pressing. We are often willing to give any and all for the sake of reaching the world until it calls for our people— our own flesh and blood. But this is the responsibility of the local church. Someone has said that the light which shines the farthest shines the brightest at home. All the churches and their people want to shine, but they often forget the law of shining. Jesus said of John the Baptist in John 5:35, "He was a burning and a shining light." The law is this—there is no shining without burning. The candle gives up the wax, the lamp gives up the fuel—God gave up His Son, and we must be willing to give up ourselves if world evangelism is to become a reality. There can be no shining around the world if there is not some giving up at home.

One night off our Florida coast a tempestuous gale was blowing. The violence of the wind was so terrific that it broke the glass out of one side of a large lantern in the top of the lighthouse which was set to guard the ships from the rocky coast. The keeper had no other glass with which to cover the gap and shield his lantern light. Doing his best he covered the space of the broken glass with a sheet of tin.

In this true story, there was a desperate ship beaten by the storm and whose captain sought to find the light he knew was there to help him. Not finding the light, the captain became confused and ran his vessel onto the rocks. The ship with all hands was lost and perished in the sea. Why? Because the light was not allowed to shine.

The church must be willing to take its hands off its children, its youth, its adults, and give them up—praying God to call them to the mission field of world evangelism. Notice I carefully selected my words. I did not say that the church should be *willing* for these people to go, but I said we should *pray to God* to call them to go. It is one thing to be willing to let someone go if God calls them, but it is altogether a different matter to be actively praying that God will in fact call someone to go.

Recently this was dramatically made clear to me. My wife and I have two children who are very loving and affectionate. The girl, being old enough to be more sensitive, seems to be a bit more affectionate. One night as I prayed in a motel room, thanking God for the love and affection of these two children toward their mother and me, I began to wonder, *Why are they so affectionate?* Immediately the thought came: *Perhaps my wife and I were getting in advance what later we would not have because of the absence of our children.* I began to say to God, "Lord, you know I am willing for my children to go anywhere you call them."

Then God seemed to say to me, "But do you really *want* me to have them to go anywhere?" I felt like the rich young ruler must have felt as Jesus put his finger down on the most tender part of the young man's existence—"because he had great possessions."

There on my knees, with tears washing my face, I said, "Dear Lord, I've been willing, but I have not really *wanted* you to call my own flesh and blood away from me for the cause of the gospel— but Jesus, I am ready now!"

Since that time I have had a willingness and a want for God to call out of our church our best, and one by one God is moving in an unusual manner with that distinctive tap on our hearts calling people to world evangelism.

Our churches must be willing to give up if there is going to be any real giving out of the gospel around the world. There will be no shining without burning!

My heart was caught by a little tract that had

no copyrights and was only one page, consisting mainly of a real-life illustration, "Dr. Duff's Appeal." Dr. Alexander Duff, that great veteran missionary to India, returned to Scotland to die, and as he stood before the general assembly of the Presbyterian Church, he made his appeal, but there was no response. In the midst of his appeal he fainted and was carried off the platform. The doctor bent over him and examined his heart. Presently Duff opened his eyes.

"Where am I?" he cried. "Where am I?"

"Lie still," said the doctor. "You have had a heart attack. Lie still."

"But," exclaimed Dr. Duff, "I haven't finished my appeal. Take me back. I must finish my appeal."

"Lie still," said the doctor again. "You will go back at the peril of your life."

But, in spite of the protests of the physician, the old missionary struggled to his feet, and with the doctor on one side and the moderator of the assembly on the other side, he again mounted the steps of the pulpit platform. As he did so, the entire assembly rose to do him honor. Then, when they were seated, he continued his appeal, and this is what he said:

"When Queen Victoria calls for volunteers for India, hundreds of young men respond, but when King Jesus calls, no one goes."

Then he paused. There was a silence. Again he spoke:

"Is it true," he asked, "that the fathers and mothers of Scotland have no more sons to give for India?"

Again he paused. Still there was silence.

"Very well," he concluded, "then, aged though I am, I'll go back to India. I can lie down on the banks of the Ganges and I can die and thereby I can let the people of India know that there was one man in Scotland who loved them enough to give his life for them."

In a moment young men all over the assembly sprang to their feet, crying, "I'll go!" And after the old white-haired preacher had been laid to rest, these young men, having graduated, found their way to dark benighted India, there to labor as his substitutes for the Lord Jesus Christ.

Do you remember when the Lord Jesus Christ fed the five thousand? Do you recall how he had them sit down, row upon row, on the ground? Then do you remember how he took the loaves and fishes and blessed them and then broke them and gave them to his disciples? And do you remember how the disciples started at one end of the front row and went right along that front row giving everyone a helping? Then do you remember how they turned around and started back along that front row again, asking everyone to take a second helping? Do you remember?

No! A thousand times, no! Had they done that, those in the back rows would have been rising up and protesting most vigorously. "Here," they would

have been saying, "come back here. Give us a helping. We have not had any yet. We are starving; it
isn't right; it isn't fair. Why should those people
in the front row have a second helping before we
have had a first?"

And they would have been right. We talk about
"the second blessing." They haven't had the first
blessing yet. We talk about the second coming of
Christ. They haven't heard about the first coming
yet. It just isn't fair. "Why should anyone hear the
gospel twice before everyone has heard it once?"
You know, as well as I do, that not one individual
in that entire company of five thousand men, be-
sides women and children, got a second helping
until everyone had had a first helping.

I have never known a minister to have any trouble with the back rows. All his trouble comes from
the front rows. Those in the front rows are overfed,
and they develop spiritual indigestion. They tell
him how much to feed them; when to feed them;
when to stop feeding them; how long to feed them;
what kind of food to give them, etc., etc., and if
he doesn't do it, they complain and find fault.

My friend, I have been with the back rows. I
have seen the countless millions in those back
rows famishing for the Bread of Life. Is it right?
Should we be concentrating on the front rows?
Ought we not rather to be training the front rows
to share what they have with the back rows, and
thus reach the back rows with the gospel, those
for whom nothing has been prepared?

I thing we should. I think they, too, have a right to hear. What, then, are we going to do about it? Has God spoken to them? Have you heard his call? Will you cry out, "I'll go! I'll go!" And, if you cannot go, will you send a substitute? Will you put your money into a printed page? Will you do something for the back rows? It is for you to decide.

Money Provisions

Money provisions must be given if the people with the gospel are to reach those without the gospel. We once pictured our missionaries in shorts, sunburned, wearing white pith helmets. They used walking sticks and marched out into the jungle and told natives about Jesus. They carried cameras and lights to line people up and take pictures, making sure to get properly taken film. Their best shot was the final sunset scene.

Somehow where they lived was always a very inexpensive place to live and raise a family. If you sent them a few dollars, they could turn it into much money in the country where they worked. For clothes, other than the shorts, they were to wear worn-out, out-dated items that churches shipped to them by the barrel. When they came home, they brought an old car and traveled for one year from church to church, showing slides and taking an offering just large enough to get them to the next church. Any extra money went toward boat tickets to get back over "there."

Today's missionaries are far more mobile, able

to adapt quickly, and are no longer just a little unusual. God called them to serve crossculturally and they answered, giving up familiar forms for foreign ones. A great many are bilingual or multilingual. Most are highly educated. They dress like we do or as people do where they serve. Missionaries are doing what we can't do. They are taking the gospel to other nations, and learning customs and languages to avoid antagonizing or insulting. Their motive is to carry out "go into all the world and preach the gospel."

Things have changed a great deal, haven't they! The world isn't mostly jungles, and the missionaries seldom wear helmets! Furthermore, it is likely to cost more to live "overseas" than it costs you to live here. Dollars aren't very valuable any more, and it takes more of them. Missionaries now need to live on a scale much like in America because other countries have high standards of living, and if missionaries actually dressed from the boxes of old clothes, no one would listen to them. They don't travel in steamers—they fly. They aren't quaint and outdated when they come home, because TV, tapes, literature, and news reporting have put the world much more in touch. Yes, the gospel is still free, but the channels through which it passes most certainly are not free. It is the churches' responsibility to provide the offerings and money needed to spread the gospel throughout Jesus' perimeter of operation.

Let me share with you one of the most exciting

things God has led our church to do in order to
build our faith and give more to missions. We do
have missions in our budget for almost 20 percent,
but we wanted to do more and go further with
the gospel. So, in addition to our budget gifts we
entered into "Faith Promise Giving." God had laid
this on my heart primarily as a vehicle to encourage and grow our church in faith. Faith would
be the aim and giving would be the vehicle. We
called this ministry "An Adventure in Faith for
the Growing Christian." While this concept of
Faith Promise Giving is by no means original with
us, and has been greatly used of God to raise multi-
plied thousands of missionaries and mission dollars, it has most assuredly revolutionized our
church's faith giving and gospel spreading. In one
service with almost no promotion, and very little
understanding of the concept, our people committed over $ 22,000 to mission outreach via Faith
Promise, and we are giving over that amount now.

I share a few of the details because if we are
serious about Bold Mission Thrust, every avenue—
traditional or nontraditional—must be exhausted.
Faith Promise is where the believer looks to the
Lord "in faith," asking how much God would have
him give and then promises to give as the Lord
provides the gift. The Faith Promise offering is
different from a cash offering, because it requires
little if any faith to give a cash offering. If you
have a dollar in your pocket, all you have to do
is to tell your hand to go into the pocket and take

it out and put it into the plate. You don't have to ask God about it or pray about it. You don't have to trust God for any definite amount. You just have to give it.

With Faith Promise you have to pray about it and ask God how much he would have you give and then trust him for it. Then, week by week go to him in prayer and ask him to supply the amount promised and wait upon him in trusting faith until it comes in. This is the offering that grows our faith and brings the blessings.

Further, this promise is not a pledge. A pledge is horizontal, made to a church or a cause, but faith promise is vertical, being made between the believer and the Lord. No attempt is made to collect the faith promise—in fact we ask our people to sign nothing at all, so it would be impossible to know who had committed what to the Lord. If, at the end of the year, God has not enabled a person to meet his Faith Promise commitment, the matter is only between the person and the Lord.

Faith Promise is based on 2 Corinthians chapters 8 and 9 where it tells of giving "to their powers" and giving "beyond their powers." Most of us have given only in our own power, but Faith Promise calls us "beyond" any known sources of income and causes us to look by faith to the Lord for his special enabling. One of the great advantages is that it in no way affects tithes or offerings or budget giving, since they are based on known income, and Faith Promise must be on unknown income. Further, through Faith Promise, God can get 100 percent of what he desires and directs into his works.

All across the country God is using Faith Promise as a vehicle to grow the faith of his people and to add a wonderful dimension to world evangelism.

General George Patton, who was known for his ability to go deep into the enemy stronghold, had painted on the side of his army tanks three A's in a line. After the A's there was a large 0 with a slash mark through it. Someone asked this aggressive general, who had kept the enemy on the run so long, what all that meant. Patton replied, "That means we will fight anywhere, anytime, anyway, bar nothing."

This must become the spirit of the worldwide missions and evangelism in the church. That we will spread the gospel anywhere, anytime, anyway, bar nothing. World evangelism does not need sympathy—it needs action on the part of the church and the believer. Someone asked Spurgeon what he thought would happen to the heathen if the heathen never got the gospel. Spurgeon replied, "The thing that bothers me is what will happen to us if we do not supply the gospel to the heathen!"

We who are endeavoring to live in the personage of Jesus, and to be instruments in the program of Jesus, face a decision. You cannot have more righteousness in the world by having less Bible.

You cannot have more peace by having less Christ and God's program. The call of God and the cry of the world is for Christians to put the gospel into the hands, hearts, and homes of the entire world!

A stranger asked to be carried out fishing with a man who had been recently bringing in unbelievable loads of fish. Once the stranger and fisherman were way out into the water the stranger asked, "How do you catch so many fish?" At that the fisherman lit and threw into the water a stick of dynamite. When it exploded hundreds of dead fish came to the surface. The stranger said, "You, of course, know it is unlawful to catch fish in that fashion, and since I am the game warden I must arrest you."

At that the fisherman lit another stick of dynamite and pitched it to the game warden, saying, "Warden, are you going to fish like I do or just sit there with that dynamite and talk!"

Oh, Christian friend, is your heart hurting for a world that needs the touch of God's gospel? Are you hungry to see a fresh movement of God through you and your church at home and around the world? As David Livingstone said, "Sympathy can be no substitute for action." We need to decide to get serious about worldwide fishing and stop just talking.

PART IV.

THE PREVIEW OF JESUS' RETURN

1. RETURN
2. RESURRECTION
3. REUNION
4. REWARDS

THE PREVIEW OF JESUS' RETURN

"And when he had spoken these things, while they beheld, he was taken up; and a cloud received him out of their sight. And while they looked stedfastly toward heaven as he went up, behold, two men stood by them in white apparel; Which also said, ye men of Galilee, why stand ye gazing up into heaven? This same Jesus, which is taken up from you into heaven, shall so come in like manner as ye have seen him go into heaven" (Acts 1:9-11).

I relate a true happening that took place in a small Southern town. A mother and father with two small children worked hard to maintain a moderate standard of living. The two children were a girl about ten years and a boy about seven years old. The father was sick in bed and expected to die anytime, and the mother had been taken by some deathly illness.

In a distant city this mother had recently undergone some of the most specialized surgery which is available today, only to hear the doctors hopelessly tell her she had only hours to live. The mother, far away from her helpless husband and two precious children, jotted a final note and gave it to the nurse, asking, "Will you please give this to my little girl?" The nurse agreed and, as she walked down the hall, she opened the note and read the message of this dying mother to her little girl. "Honey, clean yourself up—get your brother and hurry, hurry, hurry!"

1. RETURN

Why get excited about the personage of Jesus, the program, the perimeter? Because the Bible text has promised, "This same Jesus, which is taken up from you into heaven, shall so come in like manner as you have seen him go into heaven."

Jesus really is coming back! This *Same* Jesus—not a substitute, not a likeness, not another but the "same" Jesus is coming back, and we have already witnessed the preview of his return!

Do you believe that Jesus will return even before you finish this paragraph? The Bible says, "In an hour you think not the Son of man shall come." Today would be a great day for his return!!! So then, we who love the Lord and expect his return need to be cleaned up and gathering in those around us while there is time and we need to "hurry, hurry, hurry."

God has not yet had his final say, but it is apparent that we are in the Victor's camp! God grant that we may be used to expand quickly the family of God while there is time.

In my ministry I have tried to be a verse-by-verse Bible teacher/preacher, and I, much because of this approach, have listened long and hard to many of the great expository Bible preachers. From this exposure to the Scriptures I have come to look for Jesus to return. I believe in the bodily, personal, visible, victorious, and immanent return of the Lord Jesus Christ back to this earth again. I believe those angels were correct when they quoted the above text of Acts 1:11. Further and foremost, I believe Jesus when he said, "I go to prepare a place for you. And if I go and prepare a place for you, I will come again, and receive you unto myself: that where I am there ye may be also" (John 14:2-3).

Any church that is going to be a real spiritual lighthouse with the gospel must, of necessity, grasp this wonderful doctrine and truth. Our belief in the second coming of Christ will have everything to do with the sense of urgency in our daily living, as well as the sense of urgency in our churches' ministry. If we really do believe that Christ is coming again, and soon, it will make a profound and pronounced impact on our lives and work. We will not be willing to simply wait; we will want to worship and work "as unto the Lord!"

Following are some of the elements of the future return of Christ which should motivate us here and now:

The Rapture

The word "rapture" cannot be found in the concordance of your Bible, and there is a good reason—it is not in the Bible. Someone will say, "I do not want to believe in something that is not in the Bible." I agree with that statement, but have you tried to find the Trinity in the Bible? Trinity is not in the Bible but we use that word or term to describe a very true and precious doctrine of the Father, Son, and Holy Spirit.

It is the same way with the word Rapture, which is used to describe a true and precious event when He takes the born-again persons out of this earth. The "Rapture" or "snatching away" of the children of God is to come before the period of the Tribulation and millennial (1,000 years) reign of Jesus on the earth.

Revelation 4:1-2 and 1 Thessalonians 4:16-17 give us a glimpse at this great day when Christ will call his people home. Have you ever tried to reconcile the account of the public return of the Lord (Rev. 1:7), where everyone saw it, with the private return (Matt. 24:36-44), where it happens without many knowing? How could this be so? The private return is the surprise "Rapture" or "snatching away" of the born-again children of God before the Tribulation. The public return is where Christ comes back to earth with a host of heaven for the millennial reign. But what does all this have to do with us in the here and now? It has everything! It seems that most all great out-reaching ministries and people have been those who labored and lived under the excitement and urgency of Jesus' soon coming.

Bishop Steed was a dear preacher of yesteryear. The last thing he did before retiring in the evening was to go to his window, lift the shade, raise the window, and look up to see if he might get a glimpse of Jesus coming that night. First thing he did in the morning upon rising was to go to the window, lift the shade, raise the window, look up to see if Jesus was coming.

Friend, do we want our lives to be clean and pure? Do we want to give up some sin? Do we want our lives to be a blessing to God? Do we want to have souls fresh on our heart? Do we want to be more careful about our habits? Do we want fire put into our hearts? Do we want a sense of urgency on our life's work? Do we want to hear trumpets in the morning calling us to our mission and min-istry?

Then we need to make it our habit to start seri-ously looking morning, noon, and night for Jesus' return! God has seemed always to especially bless those who have looked for the Rapture and return. The late R. G. Lee's booklet, *The Second Coming of Christ* (page 27), gives a list of such blessed men. When I read this list my heart goes back to Hebrews 12:1-2. "Wherefore seeing we also are compassed about with so great a cloud of witnesses, let us lay aside every weight, and the sin which doth so easily beset us, and let us run with patience the race that is set before us. Looking unto Jesus the author and finisher of our faith; who for the joy that was set before him endured the cross, despising the shame, and is set down at the right hand of the throne of God."

The other day I was talking with a woman on the plane and telling her how tired I got of airplane rides. She said, "I know what you mean, I am also tired of *airplane* rides, but I am looking forward to a *plane-air* ride when Jesus comes for me." If anything should urge us to get on with the program of Jesus, it should be the fact that one great day we will be caught up to meet him in the air.

2. RESURRECTION

Another important fact of Jesus' return is the resurrection.

> *But some man will say, How are the dead raised up? and with what body do they come? Thou fool, that which thou sowest*

is not quickened, except it die: and that which thou sowest, thou sowest not that body that shall be, but bare grain, it may chance of wheat, or of some other grain: But God giveth it a body as it hath pleased him, and to every seed his own body. All flesh is not the same flesh: but there is one kind of flesh of men, another flesh of beasts, another of fishes, and another of birds. There are also celestial bodies, and bodies terrestrial: but the glory of the celestial is one, and the glory of the terrestrial is another. There is one glory of the sun, and another glory of the moon, and another glory of the stars: for one star differeth from another star in glory. So also is the resurrection of the dead. It is sown in corruption; it is raised in incorruption: It is sown in dishonour; it is raised in glory: it is sown in weakness; it is raised in power: It is sown a natural body; it is raised a spiritual body. There is a natural body, and there is a spiritual body. And so it is written, The first man Adam was made a living soul; the last Adam was made a quickening spirit. Howbeit that was not first which is spiritual, but that which is natural; and afterward that which is spiritual. The first man is of the earth, earthy: the second man is the Lord from heaven. As is the earthy, such are they also that are earthy: and as is the heavenly, such

*are they also that are heavenly. And as we
have borne the image of the earthy, we shall
also bear the image of the heavenly. Now
this I say, brethren, that flesh and blood
cannot inherit the kingdom of God; neither
doth corruption inherit incorruption. Behold, I shew you a mystery; We shall not
all sleep, but we shall all be changed, In a
moment, in the twinkling of an eye, at the
last trump: for the trumpet shall sound, and
the dead shall be raised incorruptible, and
we shall be changed. For this corruptible
must put on incorruption, and this mortal
must put on immortality. So when this corruptible shall have put on incorruption,
and this mortal shall have put on immortality, then shall be brought to pass the saying that is written, Death is swallowed up
in victory. O death, where is thy sting? O
grave, where is thy victory? The sting of
death is sin; and the strength of sin is the
law. But thanks be to God, which giveth us
the victory through our Lord Jesus Christ.
Therefore, my beloved, brethren, be ye sted-
fast, unmovable, always abounding in the
work of the Lord, forasmuch as ye know
that your labour is not in vain in the Lord
(1 Cor. 15:35-58).*

The teaching and the preaching of the resurrection almost consumed the ministry of the apostles.

As a matter of fact, the apostles almost abandoned the preaching of Christ's death for the preaching of the resurrection as can be seen in over forty New Testament passages which refer to the resurrection. It is almost always taught as a literal resurrection and raising of the physical body.

One of the joys of being a child of God is to know we really never die. Our souls do not ever die. Our earthly body is like a space suit used by the astronauts. The astronauts put on the space suit because it would allow them to dwell and be best suited for another environment of outer space. And so it is with our soul in relationship to earthly bodies. This earthly body is the space suit of the soul for this environment here on earth. We are pretty tough on some of our old earthly space suits, aren't we? Hair comes out, eyes go dim, hearing goes out, and even occasionally the limbs come off. The reason for the rough wear is because this environment is contaminated with sin, suffering, and sorrow. Now for the Christian, who is headed for paradise and heaven at death, God has a new "space suit" tailor made for that environment; the Bible calls it a glorified body. It is perfect for the environment of heaven which is glorious. This is glorious!

But I would not have you to be ignorant, brethren, concerning them which are asleep, that ye sorrow not, even as others which have no hope. For if we believe that Jesus died and rose again, even so them also which sleep in Jesus will God bring with him. For this we say unto you by the word of the Lord, that we which are alive and remain unto the coming of the Lord shall not prevent them which are asleep. For the Lord himself shall descend from heaven with a shout, with the voice of the archangel, and with the trump of God: and the dead in Christ shall rise first: Then we which are alive and remain shall be caught up together in the clouds, to meet the Lord in the air: and so shall we ever be with the Lord. Wherefore comfort one another with these words (1 Thes. 4:13-18).

Comfort is the big word that stands out in the last verse of the text above and how we need it today. The resurrection should be a blessing and a comfort to those who love and labor for the Lord.

I preached a funeral of a nine-year-old boy who had tragically drowned. The family was, for a few moments, at the casket. The mother became hysterical. Different people tried to help this poor mother. Then with all the care in the world the funeral director began to quote softly the text about the resurrection from 1 Thessalonians 4:13-18. Suddenly the woman had a peace about her that was unbelievable. The resurrection hope had had its effect.

A man told about getting lost while out hunting and came to a farmhouse for information. A young boy told him, "Mister, go down this road to the creek and then follow the creek to your right through the woods. When you come out of the woods you will see a graveyard. Go right through the middle of the graveyard, and when you go on the other side of the graveyard your troubles will be over and you can see the way clearly."

That is it, isn't it? Comfort comes in knowing that life just begins and troubles are left behind on "the other side of the graveyard." Do you want to comfort somebody who is about to die? Do you want to comfort someone who is downtrodden? Do you want to comfort someone who is broken-hearted, bereaved, or empty? Then tell them that Jesus is coming and that the resurrection is real and therein is comfort. Remind them that, for the Christian, there will be no more pain; there will be no more suffering; there will be no more sorrow; there will be no more heartaches. There will be no more sickbeds.

Not only should the resurrection give us comfort for our own lives and that of other believers but should give us concern for those who are not believers.

In years past New York City had an epidemic of suicides. Careful study was made of these suicide cases, and it was concluded that these people had everything to live *with* but nothing to live *for.*

This should be our point of concern.

I was leaving the bedside of a young man named Jerry. He told me that a few days before, when he almost died, he had talked with the Lord. Jerry just knew that he was ready to die and go be with the Lord. But he went on to tell me of all the problems in his home, marriage, and even his Christian journey. Then he said, "Brother Welch, I know I am ready to die but tell me how I can keep on living." The answer to that is, of course, *in Jesus* and the fact that this earthly existence is only a very small part of our eternal existence. In light of eternity, the return of Christ, the Rapture and the resurrection, any pain, sorrow, labor, or suffering is just temporary.

The resurrection is a promise of hope to the Christian, but it is exactly the opposite to the lost person who goes beyond the graveyard without Jesus as Lord and Savior. The Bible tells of the resurrection of damnation. "They that have done evil unto the resurrection of damnation" (John 5:29).

"But the rest of the dead lived not again until the thousand years were finished. This is the first resurrection" (Rev. 20:5).

And I saw a great white throne, and him that sat on it, from whose face the earth and the heaven fled away; and there was found no place for them. And I saw the

*dead, small and great, stand before God;
and the books were opened; and another
book was opened, which is the book of life:
and the dead were judged out of those
things which were written in the books, according to their works. And the sea gave
up the dead which were in it; and death
and hell delivered up the dead which were
in them: and they were judged every man
according to their works. (Rev. 20:11-13).*

What does this say to you? It says to me that I
should be comforted by those that are saved and
concerned by those that are still lost. The Bible
tells that eternity is for the lost and an eternity
in the lake of fire. Who can imagine that? Being
in a place where the soul and body continue in
torment forever and forever. Man who lives a life
of sin and Christlessness is going to be destined
for the consequences of such a life. Revelation 6:7
says, "Whatsoever a man soweth, that shall he also
reap." There is no exception to this. Some seem
to violate this law but that only lasts for a while.
Finally the Scriptures come true. "Be sure your
sins will find you out."

Someone asked, "Where is hell?" Another replied, "Hell is at the end of a Christless life." That
makes me concerned for my friends and family
and the world around me. The first two people I
ever baptized were my mother and brother. Over

and over how I wanted to witness to them. I was not experienced in personal work and sharing my faith, and I had never been in any class to help me. For over six weeks, again and again I would almost do it, but then something would always hold me back. There was one thing that caused me to keep on keeping on until finally I did share, and they did pray to receive Christ. Yes, I did love them or they never would have been on my heart to begin with, but the thing that kept me coming back was that I believed hell is real and lost people go there to exist in torment forever. Who is it that you love? Who is it that you perhaps don't even like? Regardless of any of our feelings, surely there is no one we are willing to allow to go headlong into hell. The second coming, the Rapture, the resurrection, eternity, heaven and hell should call us to concern for the lost.

It is not God's plan nor is it his will that "any should perish" (2 Pet. 3:9). Man voluntarily chooses the way of God or the way of Satan, and will belong to one or the other, but not to both. "No man can serve two masters: for either he will hate the one, and love the other; or else he will hold to the one, and despise the other. Ye cannot serve God and Mammon. Therefore I say unto you, Take no thought for your life; what ye shall eat, or what ye shall drink; nor yet for your body, what ye shall put on. Is not the life more than meat, and the body more than raiment?" (Matt. 6:24-25).

If a man has chosen God he will love him and

follow him to heaven. If a man belongs to the devil he will love his ways and follow him to hell. God does not send men to hell, but they choose their own place. Judas said he loved Jesus but he served and followed Satan and the Bible says, "that he might go to his own place" (Acts 1:25).

Our part as we look to the end of time, whether it be by death or the Rapture and second coming, is to persuade men in the power of God's Spirit to follow Christ. We do that because we love souls and are concerned. Dear God, may your Son's coming and the reality of eternity and heaven or hell make us urgently concerned!

A deputation had called at Number 10 Downing Street to ask the help of the great prime minister. Gladstone was busy in an upstairs apartment when they arrived and, until he could be reached and free to see them, his wife entertained the people downstairs. Being so full of their troubles they began to pour them out to her. The spokesman said at last, ending the long recital with a pious declaration: "Well, anyway, there is One above who will be able to put everything right!" Mistaking their meaning Mrs. Gladstone replied, "Yes, and he will be down any minute now." The Bible tells us God came down with the law of life at Sinai. He came down with the gift of life at Bethlehem. He came down with the power of life at Pentecost. But at his second and last coming he will come down with eternal life.

3. REUNION

I get excited about the coming of the Lord because of those I am going to meet again. We often
say and speak of one who has died and gone on
to be with the Lord as one we have "lost." But if
they were saved and we are saved, we have not
lost them, because we know exactly where they
are, and one day we, too, will join them.

I can remember as a child how death frightened
me. To die would have been the worst possible
thing. I did not want any part of it and did not
want to talk of it. You were probably the same
way. But now things have changed. One reason
my view of death has changed is because I am
secure in my eternal salvation. Another important
reason is because of the investment I now have
in heaven.

When I was a child none of my loved ones had
died and gone to heaven, so I had little interest
in death and the beyond. But since those days of
my childhood I have made a number of slow walks
from the funeral parlor to the cemetery with those
I loved so dearly. It seems now that as more of
my earthly treasures get placed there in heaven
the more I look forward to that great reunion. God
has been unbelievably good to me and blessed me
beyond measure. Through these years I have re-

ceived a lot of plaques, distinguished awards, several rows of medals for combat in the military, and the Lord has allowed me to have a good education.

But you know what? I would be willing to pile all those things into the nearest garbage can and never see their likes again if I could trade them for one small black-and-white picture of my father and me together in the house of the Lord in worship. I will never get that black-and-white picture here because he was saved only a short time before his death.

But I know I will get to be with him at the feet of Jesus when that reunion takes place. My wife's father died when she was very small, and my father died ten years ago. On a recent evening my wife and I were talking about how good it would be to see them again. And the glorious part of it is that we surely will! Don't you have someone waiting there? If those around you died today, would they be waiting there? Oh, when we see the reality of that reunion day we will get a sense of urgency about us for those around us.

A mother after the evening meal found her little girl standing at her bedroom window. The girl was dressed in her very best dress and shoes. She gazed through the window into the sky. "Honey, why are you all dressed up?" asked the mother.

"Well, you and Daddy were talking at supper about Jesus coming back anytime. So I hurried and took my bath and got dressd in my best outfit because I wanted to look nice and be ready when he comes."

And I do want to look nice, be nice, and be ready for that great reunion day! That puts a sense of urgency in my life.

4. REWARDS

It is certainly true that we should love and serve the Lord just because he is who he is. However, it is just as true that God, in his providential planning of the ages, is pleased to give heavenly rewards to faithful followers. To any sincere follower of Christ there should be a Godly desire to be a recipient of these rewards in heaven.

Many, many people have had the false idea that at the end of time every person who has ever lived will line up before a Great White Throne to be judged. This idea gives the impression that each one takes a turn, one standing and waiting for his verdict, whether he will go to heaven or hell. This teaching and idea is totally foreign to the Bible.

While there is a Great White Throne judgment, it has nothing to do with the Christian whatsoever, since the Christian will not even be present for that particular judgment. What determines whether a person goes to heaven or hell is based upon receiving Jesus or rejecting him as Lord, and that is settled here on earth, not after death. The Great White Throne judgment is the final judgment because it takes places after the millennial reign of Christ. "But the rest of the dead lived not again until the thousand years were finished. This is the first resurrection" (Rev. 20:5). "And I saw the dead, small and great, stand before God; and the books were opened: and another book was opened, which is the book of life: and the dead were judged out of those things which were written in the books, according to their works. And the sea gave up the dead which were in it; and death and hell delivered up the dead which were in them; and they were judged every man according to their works" (Rev. 20:12-13). This is the time of judgment upon the unsaved person's evil works and deeds (Rev. 20:12). This will be a time of final consignment of the lost person to eternal hell (Rev. 20:15). This then is in general the eternal reward of those who reject Christ.

There are the records and rewards for the believer, as well as the non-believer. Immediately after the Rapture of a born-again person, there is going to be judgment of the saved. Remember this is not to determine salvation—that was done on earth at the receiving of Jesus as Lord and Savior. There will, of course, be no unsaved souls at this judgment.

First Corinthians 3:9-15 gives us some detail as

to the judgment of Christians. This is referred to as the *bema* judgment because in the Greek athletic games there would be a platform and/or seat on which the ruler of the game sat and awarded the winner. This word is fitting in the New Testament description of the Christian's judgment of his works and deeds done in the body. John 5:22 and Romans 14:10 indicate that God has turned this judgment seat responsibility over to his Son. As we individually stand before Jesus, one by one, our works will be judged as to whether they were acceptable or unacceptable to God. Things done for our benefit and glory, even though they may have been done in or under the name of the Lord, will be disapproved. Those things done for the glory of the Lord and for him alone will be approved and rewarded.

In the New Testament there are five things that seem to be the grounds for heavenly rewards. (1) Soul-winning (1 Thes. 2:19), (2) The love of Jesus' second coming (2 Tim. 4:8), (3) Enduring trials (James 1:12), (4) Victory over the old nature (1 Cor. 9:25), and (5) Feeding the flock (1 Pet. 5:4).

Rewards are given for these different areas of the Lord's service so we might use the rewards and crowns to lay before God in glory.

I do not know what the world is coming to, but I know who is coming to the world. And because Jesus at his coming is going to judge us for our works and reward us, in order that we might glorify the Father, we should want to be found urgently at work "as unto the Lord." Dr. Jerry Vines, in his sermon on the ascension of Jesus, told a story of a Christian children's home for retarded boys and girls somewhere in Kentucky. They teach them the Word of God there.

They simply cannot keep the window panes of the home clean. Do you know why? Those little children keep their noses and faces and hands on the windows day after day. They are looking for that blessed hope! Let me ask you something—do you stand at the window panes of your heart looking for Jesus? Do you serve in your church, love your Lord, witness for souls, looking for that blessed hope?

Last night there was a hard rain. This morning at the breakfast table my little girl asked me, "Daddy, did you look out the window at the sky this morning?" Then she went on to add, "I don't mean at the weather, but for that something special—Jesus' coming—it would be a good day for it, wouldn't it, Daddy?" I was so happy to say, "Yes, honey I did look out the window for him this morning and yes, it would be a great day for him to come!"

"Even so, come, Lord Jesus."

PART V.

THE POWER OF JESUS' CHURCH

1. VISION

2. VITALITY

3. VICTORY

THE POWER OF JESUS' CHURCH

"Then returned they unto Jerusalem from the mount called Olivet, which is from Jerusalem a sabbath day's journey. And when they were come in, they went up into an upper room, where abode both Peter, and James, and John, and Andrew, Philip, and Thomas, Bartholomew, and Matthew, James the son of Alphaeus, and Simon Zelotes, and Judas the brother of James. These all continued with one accord in prayer and supplication, with the women, and Mary the mother of Jesus, and with his brethren" (Acts 1:12-14).

In the English countryside thousands of Christians converged on a small building in the marshes just outside a lonely little town. It looked more like a barn than a church, but a church it was, and a church it has been for 1,300 years. The reporter covering the event told how proud the villagers were, both of this, one of the oldest churches in England, and also of the brand-new atomic power station that was built there. But, added the Christian villagers, the atomic power station is scheduled to last only twenty-four years. The Christian power station has survived for thirteen centuries, and it will be there when the other one is forgotten.

That is a potent concept of the Christian church—as a power station; but the question is, is it true? It clearly was true in those far-off days of the New Testament when a handful of amateur missionaries and soul-winners won great tracts of the Roman Empire for Jesus Christ. So dynamic a power force was their faith that even an experienced magician like Simon would come to the Christians and say to them, "Give me also this power." Christianity obviously was something of grand and great power: people saw it and sensed it. Yes, it was true then, that the church was a power station; and it is true in some parts of the world today.

I have heard accounts of phenomenal growth and movement of God among a group of believers in South America. These are reaching utterly illiterate people; they are staffed by clergymen, if you can call them that, who spend all their week's time working in an ordinary job. They are indigenous churches; they do not rely on foreign money to keep them going. They meet for fellowship, instruction, and testimony—not once a week, but every night. They preach and teach on the street corners and in personal conversation with their friends and acquaintances. They talk boldly about

Jesus Christ. Poor though they are, these people give to the utmost of their ability. Here is a growing church. Here is a lay church. Here is a power station!

There is not one of us who would yield when it comes to our love for the Bible. I love the Word of God and most Christians I know do also. It is the inerrant and infallible Word of God for all faith and practice. But still the Bible is not enough. Never in the life of the world has there been more Bible preaching and teaching as there is today. From pulpits, radio, television, the Word of God is being preached seemingly everywhere today. Why then, in the midst of all the Bible preaching and teaching, are we seeing decline, failure, and barrenness? Look at the altars, the prayer rooms, and the baptistries—*empty!*

What has happened, I ask? Why doesn't all this Bible teaching and all these sermons do for the ungodly what the same truth did for the ungodly in the New Testament accounts? That is the big question before us today. There is enough light shed to light an unsaved man all the way to damnation, but there is not enough power present to lift that same man unto salvation.

God has not changed. Surely he is as anxious for the redemption of man today as He ever was. The gospel is the same with power unto salvation. Human hearts have not changed. The only answer to the big question is—we need *power.*

The church is filled with consecrated and untiring workers. These are brave folks and a great blessing to any and many groups. But they trust in their own works and do not have the dynamic and power on their lives and consequently do not see New Testament results.

In the focal passage from Acts 1:12-14 it is obvious that something had happened in the hearts, lives, and desires of these who assembled in order to become the power station of the living Lord.

Catherine Booth, wife of General William Booth of the Salvation Army and herself a soul-winning evangelist, said this in the midst of a London revival meeting in 1880: "I would rather have a little child with the power of the Holy Spirit, hardly able to put two sentences of the Queen's English together, to come help, bless, and benefit my soul than I would to have the most learned divine in the British Empire without it, 'for it is not by might, nor power, but by my Spirit.' When you experience that, you will lay hold upon God." It is not by any kind of might of intelligence, organization, unified efforts, eloquence, or position. It is by the power of God, and that is what is needed today.

Can we have this power equal with the early disciples and church? Yes, we can because we are in just as much need as they were. We have no better soul-winners, Christians, or preachers than those of the New Testament. They needed power and God gave it. We need power, and I believe God is giving it and will give it.

Let us look at a case study that so clearly outlines

the divine development of power and victory upon a believer's life, and consequently upon Jesus' church. From Paul's experience on the Damascus road we can see God's hand of power move in and upon a life and ministry.

> *At midday, O king, I saw in the way a light from heaven, above the brightness of the sun, shining round about me and them which journeyed with me. And when we were all fallen to the earth, I heard a voice speaking unto me, and saying in the Hebrew tongue, Saul, Saul, why persecutest thou me? it is hard for thee to kick against the pricks. And I said, Who art thou, Lord? And he said, I am Jesus whom thou persecutest. But rise, and stand upon thy feet: for I have appeared unto thee for this purpose, to make thee a minister and a witness both of these things which thou hast seen, and of those things in the which I will appear unto thee; Delivering thee from the people and from the Gentiles, unto whom now I send thee, To open their eyes, and to turn them from the darkness to light, and from the power of Satan unto God, that they may receive forgiveness of sins, and inheritance among them which are sanctified by faith that is in me. Whereupon, O king Agrippa, I was not disobedient unto the heavenly vision (Acts 26:13-19).*

1. VISION

The key to all that happened in Paul's Godly life began with what he calls in verse 19 "a heavenly vision," to which Paul further testifies he was not "disobedient." One great preacher said, "The difference between mediocrity and greatness in the work of our Lord is but one thing—VISION." We must have a generation of preachers, teachers, and workers who have a vision of seeing the world coming to Christ.

Proverbs 29:18 is most familiar to us when it declares, "Where there is no vision, the people perish." But do not allow your familiarity with this passage to rob you of its importance. Here is a solemn word for a solemn time. We live in tremendous days, days of discovery and advance when men reach for the very stars and widen their horizons on every side.

Yet they are solemn days, for while we live on the edge of an atomic volcano, the world population increases with explosive force, yet multimillions live undernourished and die unevangelized. For much of this need there is deep concern and vision in the hearts of many who are not Christians. What vision have we? We read in 1 Samuel 3:1 of how there was "no open vision." The realities of the spiritual world were hidden so that men failed to see beyond the phenomena of life into the real world of God. Spiritual blindness had over-taken them. The high priest, Eli, old and sightless, was symbolic of the spiritual state of the people. Eli, Samson, King Zedekiah and the Laodicean church were all blind and all represented the end of an era. There is always the danger that the church may slowly lose her eyesight.

The Word of God was rare. "There was no open vision." In effect, God was not speaking, people were not being enlightened; consequently there was spiritual and moral darkness everywhere. It can be like this with us. As when darkness or mist comes and all objects are blurred, or when sight is faulty, there is a haze—so may it be in the soul. God is not real. He does not seem to speak or show himself, the Scriptures dim their light, and every-thing spiritual is out of focus. We are like the world of Creation, dark and chaotic, until the Spirit of God moves and there is light.

One book of the Old Testament more than any other is a book of vision. It is Ezekiel. You will notice it begins with the prophet saying that he "saw." Prophets were called "seers" for the simple reason that they "saw" what others did not. They saw behind and into things with spiritual percep-tion. And this is what we need today—Christians who see.

In the first chapter we read that Ezekiel had "vi-sions of God." Not one but many. We need a contin-ual vision of God, for it is always our vision, our conception, and understanding of him that determines all else. Where there is no vision of God, there is no disintegration.

For Ezekiel the vision meant that behind the events of the day and the movement of contemporary history he saw God at work, acting with purpose in sovereignty and judgment. He saw God ruling over all things, directing all things. The natural man does not see this. To him events are the results of cause and effect or are haphazard. He thinks of "blind fate," he sees men manipulating their own affairs. He may, as many do today, repudiate any idea of God who is beyond and yet who controls. But this is what the Scripture reveals: this is what we see when God himself enlightens us, and it alters everything, as it did for Ezekiel.

The vision had profound effect on the prophet, for it humbled and broke him and brought him to the feet of the One he had seen, to lay strengthless until the Spirit of God "entered into him." So it is always. When we see the Lord, we are broken, only to be filled afresh with the Holy Spirit of God. And if I may add my testimony—it is that my greatest need is to see Jesus Christ and go on seeing Him.

Another of Ezekiel's many visions is found in Chapter 37, where he was shown a great valley full of dry bones. He saw Israel as they were without God, and we need to see people around us as they are without God, ruins and relics of a fallen race. They were many and very dry. How many there are in this day of population explosions! How dry is their life without God! We need to see them— as Jesus saw Lazarus, dead and decaying: Bartimaeus, blind and poor; Magdalene, passion-torn; Zacchaeus, lost; the crowds hungry and wandering, as sheep without a shepherd.

We need to see men as they can be when grace has touched them, to see Cephas in Simon, Paul in Saul and Israel in Jacob, to see men moved by the Spirit of God, made alive and new, changed, joined together, made into a living army of God, as the prophet saw bones made into battalions.

A Voice from Hell

You lived next door to me for years!
We shared our dreams, our joys and tears,
A friend to me you were indeed—
A friend who helped me when in need.
My faith in you was strong and sure;
We had such trust as should endure.
No spats between us ever rose;
Our friends were like and so our foes.
What sadness, then, my friend to find
That after all, you weren't so kind,
The day my life on earth did end,
I found you weren't a faithful friend
For all those years we spent on earth,
You never talked of my second birth.
You never spoke of my lost soul,
And of Christ Who'd make me whole
I plead today from Hell's cruel fire,

And tell you now my last desire.
You cannot do a thing for me,
No words today my bonds will free
But do not err, my friend again,
Do all you can for souls of men.
Plead with them quite earnestly
Lest they be cast in Hell with me.

Author unknown

It is from such a vision of souls that power comes and things are born. Hudson Taylor saw behind the thousands of Brighton, the millions of China. The vision gripped him. He saw them like vast valleys of dry bones. But he saw what God could and would do—and the China Island Mission was born. Oh, we must see the world as God sees it! If we have no vision, the people will perish. Ezekiel had a final vision of a city and a Temple, both of which are illustrations of the church. It began in Chapter 40, where he was told to "set his heart on all he was shown, that he might declare it to others."

What is our vision of the church? Do some of us spend time "playing at church," as children do? Are we engaging in a pastime, running our committees, planning our services, and building up our organizations? Is it all so much human endeavor in which we have never seen the church as the apostles saw it?

The church is something God must show us, as He showed Ezekiel. We must see it as it exists in the mind of God and is set forth in the New Testament. Ezekiel saw a Temple built together according to God's pattern: he saw the Prince entering it, the glory of God filling it; he saw a river flowing from it, the streams of which brought life and healing wherever it went. He saw the name of the city to be Jehovah-Shammah, meaning, "The Lord is there."

That is the church! It is a ransomed, regenerated body of people, who are cleansed from sin and built together spiritually by the indwelling of God, a people among whom God lives and reigns, out from whom there flows a river of life and love and peace and truth. It is not something *we* organize, but that *God* builds. It is a wonderful, glorious thing, a heavenly city, a Temple for the Lord Himself.

Where there is no vision, the people perish. This is the vision we need. Communists have their vision. Humanists have theirs. Heretical sects have theirs. Their vision is their passion. Have you any vision—of God, for God? Oh Lord, open mine eyes, that I may behold! Oh Lord, let there be light! Lord, that I may receive my sight!

The Vision of Ourselves

We talked of passion earlier, but let me say one thing about compassion as we think of ourselves and our vision. John Smith, the outstanding Wesleyan preacher, said once, "I am a brokenhearted man, not for myself, but on account of others: my

God has given me such a sight of the value of precious souls, that I cannot live if souls are not saved. Oh, give me souls, or else I die" (*Intercessory Prayer* by J. G. McClure, Chicago, Illinois: Moody Press, p. 115). Someone else has said, "Heaven is not moved by oratory, but it will be moved by soul agony in tears." And Spurgeon adds, "Nothing is so eloquent with the Father as his child's cry; yes, there is one thing more mighty still, and that is when a child is so sick it is past crying, and lies moaning with a kind of moan which indicates extreme suffering and intense weakness. Who can resist that moan?"

Yes, it is very true, even in getting the vision of God clearly focused in our souls requires us to see ourselves as we should be—with compassionate relationship to a lost and dying world. G. Campbell Morgan was talking about the Bible relationship of vision to the individual when he said, "When the Spirit, revealing the will of God for the world, creates in the heart a great pain and great discontent, do not let us check it. This is what Christian men and women, alas, are constantly doing. This is to grieve the Spirit indeed. We ought to be ready to bring the new sensitiveness of our Christian life into close touch with the world's agony until we feel its pain as our very own." (*Practice of Prayer,* G. Campbell Morgan, Baker Book House, 1960, Fleming H. Revell Co. New York, page 59).

You see, a vision is exactly what caused us to

get saved—we saw ourselves as we really were, and we saw Jesus as he really is. That eye-opening vision caused us to want one thing more than anything else in the world—the power of God unto salvation!

I have heard many preachers and teachers talk of visions, but few ever tell us how to get a vision. There has been one ingredient that has stimulated my desire for a vision and power from God. It is to become sick and tired of where I am. That is what happened when I was saved—that's what happened when I committed to pray—that is what happened when I became concerned for souls to be won. I got sick and tired of my life the way it was in those areas! If you are satisfied and complacent the way you are, then you probably need to ask God to make you miserable and give you a fresh vision. Then a craving and hungering for the power to see that vision become a reality will follow. There will be no power until there is a vision which stimulates a hunger and thirst for a fresh movement of God in and through our lives.

2. VITALITY

However, even with a vision we are destined and doomed to nothing but daydreams and air castles unless there is a vitality in our lives. In Acts 26:16, Christ tells Paul to stand on his own feet and that indicates that Christ expects us to do something ourselves, and that is vitality. There must be two kinds of vitality.

There must be physical vitality for our visions to become a reality. Many Christians today have the idea that all you need to do is sit around and meditate and God is simply going to pour out all his blessings. The sad thing is that many such Christians received this idea from a pastor or staff member who was just lazy and/or confused.

Don't misunderstand—I do believe in waiting on the Lord but there comes a time to get up and go to work. Every great and lasting work I know of throughout history has come, yes, through the power of God, but vitally linked to hard work of some Christian or group of Christians. God still honors hard work! (And by the way, real prayer, sacrificial giving, and sincere soul-winning, day in and day out, and year in and year out, is some of the hardest work on the earth.)

God desires to enter into a partnership with his children—hence the term "colaborers." God has not given us a finished airplane or television set but has offered the enablement to develop these with work. In the same fashion God expects the child of God to develop blisters on his hands while bearing the stretchers which are used to carry the world to Christ. Today we have a lot of folks that are so heavenly minded that they are no earthly good. Enter into the work of Christ and the church with sleeves rolled up—hands and heart ready for sincere work in the vineyard.

However, physical vitality, and that alone, is exactly what is sending many well-meaning, sincere Christian workers to an early grave. They begin to resemble a revolving door with a lot of motion but not much forward progress. Physical vitality alone is but sounding brass and tinkling cymbals. The result will be beautiful but will not be spiritually fruitful. There will be technique but not the pull of the power of God. The winning combination is the physical vitality linked with the spiritual vitality.

The Spirit's indwelling is what allows Christ's outpouring through us. What we are able to do *for* others will be because of what the power of the Lord has done *in* us. The Holy Spirit's unction is the vitality that we need for our actions. The problem, you see, is not with the work but the worker. God does not indwell the work but the worker. God does not anoint and bless the work, but he anoints and blesses the worker. The vitality that is a must for God's work today is not more organizations endowed with enthusiasm, but organisms indwelt with the power of the Holy Spirit.

Many Christians are in the same condition as those men of Ephesus who said, "We have not so much as heard whether there be any Holy Ghost" (Acts 19:2). Little wonder the church is weak and powerless in its impact. Many Christians are trying hard to live the Christian life, struggling hard to serve God, but it is impossible unless we rely upon the empowering Holy Spirit. Let us establish three key facts that are foundational for spiritual vitality in the Holy Spirit. (1) The Holy Spirit is a person and is the third person in the Trinity. (2) The Scriptures are clear to teach that the Holy Spirit indwells every child of God. (3) The Holy Spirit as a member of the Godhead is indwelling us and is in us to make real and possible all that God has planned to be done in and through our lives individually and collectively.

This is all so important because the divine standard that God has set for Christian living and service is mighty high, so high that it is impossible to reach, except by this power of the Holy Spirit. No amount of brightly polished organizational machinery can ever take the place of unctionizing action. What is this action of unction that we can expect of the Holy Spirit's power?

It is the work of the Holy Spirit that produces the new birth (John 3:3-5). We are born again when he implants the new life in us, and from that moment on the very life of the risen Lord begins to rise within us. Jesus is on the throne and he is our life. The Holy Spirit conveys his life to us when we are born again. He is the vine; we are the branches; his life flows from him into us. He is the sap of life which rises up within us and the One Who imparts this new life to us, extends it within us, and transmits it through us.

He is not only the sap but the Holy Spirit is the seal of our assurance (Eph. 1:13; 14:30). A seal is the mark of ownership, and it speaks of safety and security. Slaves were marked to show their ownership, that they were the property and the responsibility of a certain person who would keep them safe. God has marked us off as his own and has given us the assurance that because his mark is upon us we belong to him and are safe in his keeping (Rom. 8:15–17).

The Holy Spirit is also the secret to the victorious Christian life. This Christian life is the life of the risen Lord Jesus lived out in our human bodies. Through his indwelling we can be victorious over sin, self, and Satan.

Further, the Christian receives his strength to serve by the enabling of the Holy Spirit. In Old Testament days God called people to serve him, and he gave them special anointings of the Holy Spirit to make them happy, radiant, and joyful people. This aspect of the Christian life is so important today and can only be fulfilled through the Holy Spirit (Gal. 5:22, Acts 5:41, Acts 16:25).

Thus it is the Spirit that gives power to the physical to make our lives, ministries, and churches productive. Through this controlling of Christ—then, and then only, will we be happy, joyful, useful, prayerful, radiant Christians—in other words, a power-full Christian. Jesus' church will be power-full, not because of any power in or of ourselves, but because of his power in us—"that the power of Christ may rest upon me" (2 Cor. 12:9). His power in us!!

3. VICTORY

"To open their eyes, and to turn them from darkness to light, and from the power of Satan unto God, that they may receive forgiveness of sins, and inheritance among them which are sanctified by faith that is in me" (Acts 26:18).

The above verse tells about the victory for which Christ had given Paul his vision and vitality. Victory is had when we are found earnestly, in the Lord, seeking to accomplish his mission as our ministry. This victory can be realized in a large place of service or a small place, at home or abroad, by the intelligent or the ignorant.

Even though paganism surrounds us and dissenters invade us, the cause of Christ is a victorious cause. "And I will put enmity between thee and the woman, and between thy seed and her seed; it shall bruise thy head, and thou shalt bruise his heel" (Gen. 3:15). This prophesied that the ultimate and final victory will come when Satan is conquered beneath the heel of Christ. But there is a real and immediate victory that comes when, by the power and authority of the Father, we "tread Satan" under our feet and go after the world for Jesus. This victory is through all the weapons of warfare from the power of the new life in Christ available to "whosoever will come." This is the spiritual way to a spiritual victory that assaults the very citadel of the adversary and verse 18 says, "Open their eyes, and turn them from darkness to light, and from the power of Satan unto God, that they may receive forgiveness of sins, and inheritance among them which are sanctified by faith that is in me."

So now you say, "That's what I've been praying for and believing, but I'm about ready to give up!" Are you ready to give up as a deacon, a teacher, or director, as a prayer warrior, as the pastor?

Have you ever heard of Charlie O'Connor? Charlie was a real man who lived at the turn of the century. Charlie had a real dream. That dream was to pipe water across a great distance to a very high elevation. If he could do this it would revolutionize the lives and productivity of a gold mining mountain town. But who had ever heard of such a feat? So the people laughed and mocked and called Charlie O'Connor a fool.

O'Connor did lay the pipe and get it up to the needed elevation. The crowd came as Charlie checked his watch, waiting for the water to flow forth at just the right time he had calculated. But at the time he had determined, no water came— not a drop. The crowd really began to laugh and mock now. Charlie turned and went to his hotel room, and there put a gun to his head and ended his life. The next day on the very hour that Charlie had calculated the water to arrive the previous day, the water came gushing forth and still continues to flow. What had gone wrong? Charlie had miscalculated a time change and gave up too soon.

God's ways and thoughts are not our ways and thoughts, and too many believers give up too soon on what God is trying to do in their lives.

What is it that speaks to the need of your life? Is it the personage of Jesus? The program of Jesus? The world to be won for Jesus? The urgency of Jesus' coming? The consistent power upon the church? We know that it all must begin at the personage of Jesus in and upon our lives. Are you willing to begin afresh and anew with him today?

In the capital of California there is a statue of an early pioneer representing those few early settlers who made it through all the hardships and sickness to that then-new land. Many, many died but some made it. The pioneer statue points its finger back toward the route that was so hard but led them to this new frontier of living. At the base there is a verse going something like this:

> Give me men to match my mountains,
> Give me men to match my plains,
> Give me men with new eras of their minds
>   and new empires on their brains.

I believe God in heaven is looking to us today and in a million different ways is pointing to the world and saying to each of us:

Give me Christians to match the mountains,
Give me Christians to match the plains,
Give me Christians with new visions in their minds and nothing but victory on their brains.

And, you know, you could be just that Christian!! But remember, you have to decide *This Comes First!*